The Lady Mary

MILTON WALDMAN

The Lady Mary

A Biography of Mary Tudor
1516-1558

COLLINS
ST JAMES'S PLACE, LONDON
1972

William Collins Sons & Co Ltd

London · Glasgow · Sydney · Auckland

Toronto · Johannesburg

First published 1972

© Milton Waldman 1972

ISBN 0 00 211486 0

Set in Monotype Caslon

Made and Printed in Great Britain by
William Collins Sons & Co Ltd Glasgow

To Barbie and Herbert

Contents

List of Illustrations

Note: The author wishes to acknowledge with gratitude the help of the De Witt Library of the Courtauld Institute in directing him to the portrait of Catherine of Aragon at Petworth House and of Henry VIII in the possession of the Royal College of Surgeons; also the generous guidance of Dr. Roy Strong, Director of the National Portrait Gallery.

CHAPTER ONE

The Education of a Princess

Shortly after four o'clock in the morning of 18th February, 1516, gun and bell circulated the news from Greenwich Palace that the Queen had been delivered of a female child and that it lived. In the almost hysterical rejoicing over the second fact any warning sense of disappointment at the first subsided unnoticed. Five years had elapsed since the Queen last gave birth to a living child, and even he, with a bare month's life in him, had proved but the tantalising exception to a rule of stillbirths, the last three in succession. So abnormal a run of misfortune could not be imputed to unaided Nature. Both the Queen and her consort were in the prime of youth, he 24, she 30—the same age as the dynasty which depended on her for its survival. The inference had begun to grow frightening that supernatural hostility was bent on its extinction. To this sinister hypothesis the happy issue of the Queen's latest confinement came as the plainly heaven-sent answer. A token had been given, an heir might now be confidently awaited. As the King himself, aglow with the gratitude aptly defined as a lively expectation of favours to come, explained to the Venetian legate when the latter ventured to inject a note of condolence into his Republic's official congratulations, 'We are both young. If it was a daughter this time, by the grace of God the sons will follow.'

To the informed spectator from the future the underlying irony of the situation takes more precise shape at the christening on the fourth day. Regardless of expenditure, whether of money or Tudor skill in ceremonial, the modest church of the Friars Observant was prepared for the reception of the royal infant into its Catholic birthright. Through the tapestried, rush-strewn pavilion connecting it with Greenwich Palace passed a long procession of the chief nobility and the chivalry of England, to the light of tapers and the peal of trumpets. The Earl of Devon placed the massive silver font, brought especially from Canterbury for the occasion, within the west door, the Marquess of Dorset bore the salt and his wife the consecrated oil. At the font, as the child approached in the arms of the Countess of Surrey, waited Thomas Wolsey, the Cardinal Archbishop of York, the Duchess of Norfolk, and Catherine, Princess of Castile, representing the maternal side, to answer for it as godparents. On either side of the decorated canopy held over them during the ceremony stood the Dukes of Norfolk and Suffolk, the one the premier peer of the realm, the other the husband of the King's sister Mary, Dowager of France, for whom the child was named.

Immediately after the baptism followed the confirmation, at which the Countess of Salisbury, niece of Edward IV, a Plantagenet by birth and Pole by marriage, acted as sponsor. They went through their ritual motions and responded in unison to the heralds' concluding petition for 'Good life and long unto the right high, right noble and right excellent Princess Mary, Princess of England . . .'—Courtenay and Grey, Howard and Percy, Pole and Wolsey, unconscious that their names were already inscribed amongst the *dramatis personae* of the infant's story, to die on the block or otherwise to expiate, whether as her friends or foes, the consequences of her having been born a girl. The church itself, now so gay in its cloth of gold and the glitter of jewels on the images of the saints, was one day to be struck down by the hand of the greatest of her foes, her father, and receive loving restitution at her own.

The doomed names were to keep cropping up—first with Catherine Pole, her wet-nurse, and presently amongst the household assigned to her after she had been weaned and Mistress Pole pensioned at the beginning of 1517. The 'lady mistress' placed in charge of it, Margaret Lady Brian, escaped the common fate, however, and lived to serve the Princess Elizabeth and Prince Edward in the same capacity. She was a loyal, capable woman who won and kept the respect of the King and his successive ministers by her single-minded devotion to her charges' welfare. In some respects her task rather resembled the direction of a government department than a household, still less a nursery. The organisation over which she ruled numbered even at the beginning not less than fifty persons, divided according to function under a chamberlain, a treasurer and a clerk, and comprising ladies and gentlemen in waiting, stewards, cooks, 'garciones', valets, grooms, scullery maids, stable boy and woodbearer. The running cost of this establishment, though varying somewhat from year to year, mounted on the average to over £1,000*—a budget for which the lady mistress had not only to account but sometimes to do battle with the moods, evasions and occasional downright indigence of the royal financial machinery. In addition, she carried something of the responsibilities of a commander in the field, for the household was incessantly on the move. Even at the best of times, with the dogs devouring their food on the rush-covered stone floors and horses and men waiting hours on end in the courtyard outside, a crowded residence could not long be kept

* It is virtually impossible to compare the value of money in the early sixteenth century with its value to-day. Prices fluctuated widely, often wildly, without stable relation between commodities, or between them and wages. A very rough guess would probably give a pound of 400 years ago the value of at least fifty pounds to-day.

fit for decent occupation: a thickening smell, a sign of drooping in the more delicate inmates, and the personnel was mobilised, the enormous quantity of chattels re-packed, and the household moved off for Ditton or Hanworth or Eltham, Greenwich or Windsor, Richmond, Enfield, Woodstock or some other of the royal manors, stopping on the way if the journey were long at some gentleman's house or an abbey or convent, while the permanent staff set to work to render the evacuated residence 'sweet' again for the next tour of occupation. But now and then the plague threatened—the dreaded 'sweating sickness' of the Tudor era—and a peremptory order from King or Privy Council would set the Princess into premature and even more rapid motion.

It is difficult to estimate how much time she spent in the company of her parents during these early years. The King's court, too, seldom remained long in one place and his daughter's household ordinarily crossed its path only on the occasion of the great holidays like Christmas, Easter and Whitsun—periods which added together do not seem to comprise more than three or four months of the year. It was not that the parents were indifferent, it was simply the custom. There is evidence that Catherine took an intimate personal part in the child's elementary education and that Henry himself was responsible for the orders which at time of plague or threat of plague brought her to one of the larger palaces like Richmond or Windsor in which he himself had taken refuge. In addition there were other, special occasions of reunion, notably those of her engagements to be married.

The first of these occurred in 1518, when she was two years old. It would have occurred even earlier if the nego-tiations leading up to it had not had to be dragged out until her fiancé, the Dauphin of France, was actually born. The ceremony took place in the Queen's Presence Chamber at Greenwich. Before the throne stood the

King, on his left the papal legates, Cardinals Wolsey and Campeggio, on his right, directly in front of her mother, the Princess, 'dressed in cloth of gold, a cap of black velvet on her head, adorned with many costly jewels.' The future Bishop of London, Cuthbert Tunstall, addressed her at length in learned praise of the institution of marriage. An official then took her up in his arms while the French envoys formally asked her parents' consent to the betrothal. This being given, Wolsey 'placed on her finger a small ring, in which a large diamond was set', leaving to the Lord Admiral of France the symbolic task of slipping it down over the second joint. Alert and attentive but a little mystified, the Princess apparently misunderstood this part of the proceedings and volunteered to kiss the Admiral under the impression that he was the bridegroom. The outbreak of festivity which had preceded was then followed by another in which the King's boisterous impromptu prodigalities vied with the most sumptuous allegorical artifice to achieve the fullest demonstration of delight. But the sacred character of the event was not overlooked and religious ratification was sought and given at a service in St. Paul's Cathedral. To make assurance doubly sure Henry solemnly swore in Council that the engagement should be fulfilled when Mary was 16 on pain of excommunication and an interdict on his kingdom to be pronounced by the Cardinal Legate. The Dauphin's father, Francis I, in turn subjected himself to similar anathemas if he failed to match Henry's generous promises of dowry with the largest settlement ever enjoyed by a Queen of France. The two kings further exchanged vows to meet shortly for the renewal of their pledges and until this had been accomplished not to cut off their beards.

The last promise was duly discharged on the field of Cloth of Gold, to which Henry, after a spirited resistance to his wife's aesthetic censures, brought a round and rosy beard in witness of his good faith. Yet, despite the admiration it aroused in the ladies of the French court, it lied, for its owner had already allowed himself to be seduced into perjury. In May 1520, shortly before setting out for France, he had been visited at Dover by Catherine's nephew, the King of Spain, recently elected Holy Roman Emperor under the title of Charles V. The purpose of the visit was to dissuade Henry from honouring his word to Charles's hereditary enemy, and in the course of a few days' close bargaining agreement was reached for a concerted attack upon Francis from several quarters with the transfer of Mary's hand from the Dauphin to Charles as gage of the alliance. Uncle and nephew then separated, the latter to wait at Gravelines while the former sailed to the magnificent reception prepared for him by Francis at Ardres. Mary meanwhile, 'right merry and in prosperous health, daily exercising herself in virtuous pastimes', played hostess at Richmond in her parents' absence to several gentlemen from the French court, 'welcoming and entertaining them with goodly countenance and pleasant pastime in playing on the virginals, that they greatly marvelled and rejoiced at the same, her young and tender age considered.' They departed, filled not only with good impressions but 'strawberries, wafers, wine and hippocras in plenty,' and she receded into the nursery while her father's ministers wrote his double-dealing and her altered destiny into a formal treaty.

Presently, in June 1522, she was brought to Greenwich to meet her new fiancé. With her mother and their ladies she waited at the hall door of the palace as he mounted from the great State barge in her father's company—a somewhat stoop-shouldered young man in his early twenties, with the straw-coloured hair and grotesquely underslung jaw derived from his paternal

Habsburg ancestry. As he knelt, after the Spanish fashion, to ask his aunt's blessing he gave a first impression of shyness amounting almost to sullenness. But when, 'in great joy to see his aunt, and in especial his young cousin german the Lady Mary', the master of half Europe and the Indies concentrated the full interest of his hypnotic blue eyes upon them, the first impression was abruptly supplanted by another: of sly genius whose kinship with madness appeared to be simultaneously affirmed and denied by a humorous melancholy and an intelligence so precocious as to be practically ageless. With the six-year-old child his few brief attentions then and at Windsor, where she was taken to say farewell to him, left a memory of kindness and strength upon which she was to repose with utter confidence in the worst days of her life, though she never saw him again.

Nor did she ever see the Dauphin or the various others to whom she was promised or nearly promised by the time she was eleven. The fact in itself is not surprising. Whom she married and when were matters to be decided solely in the interests of the state; those interests were assessed in terms of the importance of the royal house to whose princes she would become wife and mother, and of the strength with which its friendship could be made secure through her person; and it was natural for the rulers of the state to chop and change according to their appraisal of the international situation. But that the chopping and changing should have been accompanied by the most sacred vows men were capable of uttering is one of the unfathomable mysteries of the period's psychology. The engagement to marry was no mere declaration of mutual intention to be withdrawn at will but, as the words affiance and betroth imply, an act of faith, a pledge given to God and binding for life unless canonically dissolved; to enter into two such engagements simultaneously was on the moral plane practically

equivalent to a contract to commit bigamy.* That sixteenth-century statesmen should have been ready to
imperil their own and other people's souls for the further-
ance of their political ends was no more than was expected
of them, a hazard of their trade. But what possible ends
they thought they were furthering is the mystery that
passes understanding. The same sturdy indifference to the
risks of eternal damnation expected of them they equally
expected of their opposite numbers abroad, and exchanged supernatural sanctions with about as much hope
of their being honoured as if they had given recognisably
false coins on the chance of having them redeemed for
good. The very violence with which Henry and Francis
piled oath upon oath revealed their despair of getting
more belief than they gave; it was like trying to catch
out a rival mathematician with an equation involving
the indefinite multiplication of zero without the smallest
prospect that he would fail to detect the fallacy. Since the
sight of a Bible aroused such instant mistrust one wonders that politicians, instead of resorting to stacks of
Bibles, did not try the effect of no Bible at all. But
possibly the sixteenth century was still too near the Middle
Ages to abandon their methods along with their spirit,
since forms die harder than faith: just as the ritual of the
tourney continued to proclaim a chivalry long grown
bogus.

Of greater interest is the effect of these proceedings
upon the child who was one day to rule England by the
light of her upbringing. However little she may have
understood at 4 or 6, by 9 or 10 the discrepancy between
precept and practice could not have escaped her. Her
religious instruction was uncommonly thorough. Drilled
in her catechism and the decalogue almost as soon as she

---

* It was such pre-contracts that Henry VIII was to allege against
Anne Boleyn and Anne of Cleves in his escapes from those two of his
matrimonial misjudgments.

could speak, she knew that God was truth and that He would not hold them guiltless who took His name in vain; and as she progressed from rote to ordered exposition, not only were the duties of honesty, purity and fidelity laid down for her but related through her unfolding intelligence to the great sacramental scheme of salvation transmitted by Christ to His Church. Somehow she had to reconcile these lessons with the conduct, on the face of it blasphemously inconsistent, prescribed for her by her elders—by a father who was both King and Defender of the Faith, by the Cardinal his chief minister who was also Legate in England for the Vicar of Christ, by a mother who under her royal robes wore the coarse grey of a Franciscan Tertiary. If they explained the meaning and importance of a reason of state, they could not explain away certain perplexities of her young conscience. Nor could they even seriously try, since Francis I continued noisily to insist that her engagement to his son was still binding and they dared not deny it lest Charles V should let them down, as in fact he did. Indeed later, when they told her at the time of her troubles that the Dauphin was about to be engaged to somebody else, she answered that she could not see how that was possible since he was already engaged to her and could not have two wives. But perhaps more vivid than any words in the child's mind would have been the two rings, the little one with the large diamond from the Dauphin and the one with the emerald they had her send to the Emperor when she was 9 enclosed with a message

'that her grace hath devised this token for a better knowledge, when God shall send them grace to be together, whether his Majesty doth keep himself as continent and chaste as she will, whereby . . . his Majesty may see that her assured love towards the same hath already such operation in her, that it is also confirmed by jealousy'—of which the emerald was the symbol— 'being one of the greatest tokens and signs of hearty love and affection.'

When Charles, after warmly reciprocating her sentiments, some months later married the Infanta of Portugal, they were able to explain, along with his need of the Infanta's money, that his engagement to herself had been lawfully dissolved. But they would have been hard put to it to set her right on the offer of her hand just previously to Francis I, the father of her remaining fiancé, or on the subsequent engagement to marry him when she reached puberty, if he were still free, or else if he were not, his younger son the Duke of Orleans, at present aged 8.

By the time the list was complete for the period prior to her adolescence there figured in it, as well as her cousin James V of Scotland, the young Duke of Cleves, the old Duke of Hungary and the paralytic Duke of Milan. Though few played any direct part in her life, none was without influence in forming her mind. As gifts from relatives in far countries might stimulate other children to learn their geography, the potential husbands presented to her notice by her elders were like object lessons in contemporary history. Like herself they were pieces, great or small, in the fragile, melodramatic and often meaningless combinations of the major European potentates—meaningless, that is, except for the populations robbed and massacred in the attempt to give each new one effect. For the child the names attached to these pieces, their appearances and disappearances, provided the most immediate and vivid chronicle possible of the times in which she lived. They would have informed her not only whether her father and the Emperor and France and the Pope were friends or enemies, but why John Zapolya was excommunicated and deprived of Hungary and why Francesco Sforza was driven from

Milan—material for a whole series of dramas with real characters of which she was one. Later, when the increasing awareness of 13 or 14 had given her a critical retrospect, those names would also reflect for her, in the relative importance of their owners, the mutations of her own individual history from princess to heiress and from heiress to presumptive bastard. And that too would have had its instructional value.

To those possible marriages, moreover, are owing nearly all the evidences of her youthful personality that her contemporaries thought to record. 'By immortal God, Master Ambassador, this girl never cries,' roared her delighted father as, aged 2, she was carried off in her nurse's arms after submitting unperturbed to the prolonged inspection and homage of a roomful of strangers; to which the diplomat nimbly responded, 'Sacred Majesty, the reason is that her destiny does not move her to tears: she will one day be Queen of France.' The explanation proved to be false, but the phenomenon remained true; as she advanced through childhood observers reported her to be grave, decorous, alert, but never under any compulsion moved to tears except the compulsion of laughter owing to the weakness of her near-sighted eyes. For it was often noticed, because of the contrast with her usual sobriety, how hearty her laughter was when it came, at a piece of buffoonery at a court entertainment, a jester's antic or sheer childish high spirits when she herself took part in a dance or charade. '*Jocundius*' as well as '*decentius*' said the King's earnest servant, Dr. Richard Sampson, of her demeanour at 9, and the lines written of her some years later, when she had little enough occasion for mirth, would probably not have been inapplicable to her as she ripened into adolescence:

> *In each of her two iyes*
> *ther smiles a naked boye,*

It would you all suffice
too see those lamps of ioye.

Others noticed, as well as the smile, a particularly affecting quality in her eyes, possibly due in part to their marked myopia, when she turned them intently upon a person addressing her. They are variously reported as dark or brown, and strikingly luminous, though from her portraits one would judge them to be nearer hazel. But any of those colours would have been sufficiently striking in conjunction with the vivid pink and white complexion which all observers ascribe to her, including Heywood in another stanza of the same poem:

Her couler comes and gose
with such a goodly grace,
More ruddye than the rose
within her lively face.

Her hair, owing to the close-fitting head-dress of the time, was not usually visible, but her father once, as she unmasked at the end of a dance given for the French matrimonial ambassadors when she was 11, 'took off her cap and the net being displaced, a profusion of silver tresses as beautiful as ever seen on human head fell over her shoulders'—a description confirmed by others, at least so far as the colour went, though it seems, according to her portraits, to have grown darker by the time she reached her twenties. The head-dress also accentuated the height of her forehead without, however, affecting the childish roundness of her face—a small face, yet more than large enough for the tiny body, which would have been scrawny had it not been noticeably graceful, and which long remained so under-developed that the expert appraisers doubted whether it would be fit in normal time for matrimony. It is not improbable, though not stated,

that her voice in childhood had the surprising depth
which later so struck everybody as it issued from her
minute person.

It is always difficult to read the mind and character of
a child from the external evidences, since so much of its
life is lived inwardly. It is particularly so in the case of a
child brought up 400 years ago in circumstances more
favourable to polite exaggeration than close observation.
Like Tudor portraits, Tudor anecdotes of royalty tended
rather to embellish than reveal. Nevertheless, if it is
impossible to accept literally the tales of her beauty,
character and accomplishments, it is equally impossible
to deny the less imposing traits universally granted her,
of steadfastness in her affections, of thoughtfulness for
others, of gravity mingled with gaiety, that made her so
engaging a child in the eyes of her elders. Time and
politics were to supply a harsh corrective to the super-
latives, but the devotion she inspired in those round her
was to survive any prospect of reward from them. On
the other hand this private devotion may itself have
served as a corrective and helped to save her from the
spoiling to which constant adulation constantly exposed
her. A Princess, an only child, she received to her face
flatteries that no child could be expected to weigh;
merely to kneel and kiss her hand was a privilege reserved for the great. And the greatest of all, her father,
the mighty figure whom other men addressed as 'Sacred
Majesty', as if he were a being semi-divine, openly
adored her with all the noisy force of his vitality and vulgarity. Time after time as an infant she appears in his
arms to be dandled and vaunted, or as a young girl led
out to be exhibited for her looks, her dress, her learning
or her music. Of the possible effect upon the child Henry
apparently never thought at all. His satisfaction in all
that pertained to him was seldom subdued, and with the
simple vanity of a man whose beauty, brains, charm and

athletic renown had kept the world in a state of applause
ever since he could remember, he desired the world to
rejoice at how much his offspring did him credit. Curiously this was the result produced upon the child, a
pride in him and not in herself except as a grateful
reflection of his pride in her. Again and again, whatever
he did to her later, a conviction of his unique grandeur
among men and of his sure affection for herself would
emerge amongst the decisive factors of her conduct under
stress.

With her view of her father her mother would have
been in essential agreement, though to his careless
exuberance she provided a salutary antidote. A firm but
discriminating upholder of the natural affections, Catherine of Aragon could admire her husband and love her
daughter without pandering to the one or pampering the
other. Sent to England at the age of 16 to marry Henry's
elder brother Prince Arthur, she brought with her,
besides a considerable dowry and other substantial
advantages, the resolution to love with all the power of
which she was capable the husband she had never seen,
according to the duty she had been taught. So far as was
possible in a married life of five months with an ailing
boy of 15 she carried out her resolution, not on her own
testimony alone: and after he died lived an irreproachable
young widow until, on her father-in-law's death in 1509,
she transferred to her new king and husband, Henry
VIII, both her dowry and her will to love. Her letters to
Spain, touched with humour as well as homesickness
as she described the court frolics with which her young
lord lightened the business of ruling, reveal how thoroughly she identified herself with his joys, his disappointments and his delight with the figure he cut in
the world, and how profoundly she was moved by his
consideration at the time of her miscarriages. But her
devotion implied no abnegation of judgment. Henry

could hope for no complaisance from her when he flaunted his mistresses at court or publicly set up his little bastard by one of them, a boy three years younger than Mary, as Duke of Richmond with the household of a Prince of Wales.

It was not her vanity that was hurt but her pride. She had no illusions about her plain, matronly face and figure or well but soberly furnished mind, but she had a very definite notion of what was due to a daughter of Aragon and Castile. This sense of race was so closely allied to her sense of right and wrong as to render the two at times virtually indistinguishable from one another: two basic elements forming the powerful compound of pride which was her gravest spiritual danger and her greatest moral strength. It was the kind of pride associated then as now with her native Spain. It underlay the assumption, paramount in the history of the sixteenth century and fully shared by Catherine, that Catholic Christianity and Spanish Catholicism were one and the same thing, which it was the sacred mission of Spain to preserve. It enabled the mistress of the English court to be a participator in and yet a detached spectator of its amusements, entering into the enjoyment yet remaining aloof from the sensuality. It not only made her hard where Henry's infidelities were concerned, but incapable of sympathising with his self-pity, still less his wounded self-esteem, when the still-born babies who followed Mary set him wondering uneasily why he of all men should fail to beget living sons—until the little Henry Fitzroy, on this point at least, brought reassurance.

Between such parents there could not but be a struggle for the child's spiritual allegiance. Neither meant it to be so; until the opening of the divorce proceedings when Mary was on the threshold of adolescence it remained unspoken and unconscious, with both parents sincerely endorsing in their attitude towards each other the injunction to honour her father and her mother. But as still-births petered out into hopeless sterility and the shaping of this only child became of the most vital concern for the future, the conflict always latent in their diversity of outlook and equal strength of will took on tension and awareness. In that conflict Catherine possessed certain distinct advantages to offset the glamour of Henry's office and his overpowering personality, not only the natural advantage of a mother but others arising out of her qualities as well as his defects. There is an anecdote to the effect that Henry, anxious to discover how far his daughter had been affected by the moral laxity of the court, set Sir Francis Brian to test her during a masked ball, and on being assured that she really 'knew no foul or unclean speeches', was so delighted to find her 'prudent and of princely spirit (that he) did ever more honour her.' The story, from one of Mary's ladies, may or may not be authentic but it is apposite. Henry undoubtedly set store by his daughter's purity, but did not know her well enough to be sure of it until he had proved it by means which, like his fond exhibitions of her, can only be attributed to thoughtless impulse. But Catherine's scrupulous vigilance, her stern criterion of what was 'princely', had made sure that no such test should find the girl wanting. She had prepared for it from the first, during the early years when she could still at intervals have the child sleep in the same room with her and hear her catechism and her Latin. In that elementary instruction the theme of purity figured largely, as it did in the school books presently provided for the child's curriculum of study. It appears in the message from the girl of 9—not, one may fairly suspect, without some form of maternal inspiration—to the Emperor offering to exchange vows for the term of their betrothal, and was to reappear with almost tragic vehemence in the letter which, from the circumstances in which it was written, amounts to Catherine's spiritual testament to her daughter.

But precept alone is a poor teacher, apt to repel a pupil naturally gay with a zest for fun and adornment. Against Henry's undisciplined affection and the attractions of his court, with its high and low revelry carried on under the licence of mask and fancy dress, Catherine's efforts to place her impress on her daughter's soul would have met with smaller success had she not been able to fortify her preaching with persuasive examples. Round her, forming a little Spanish enclave of which she was the animating cause, was a coterie of her intimate ladies, diplomats, priests and men of letters whose deportment aroused the admiration of the native beholders even when they refrained from emulating it. No less receptive than their hosts to the appeal of entertainment, no less addicted to the tourney and the chase, these visitors afforded a living illustration of the proud intactness of body and spirit which Catherine's homilies endeavoured to impart. No scandal touched them since they neither provoked nor promoted it. Of the ladies who had accompanied Catherine from Spain few returned there because they were so eagerly sought as wives by the more fastidious among the English nobility. The very serving women after their training with her seldom lacked for willing husbands, to the sometimes cruel disappointment of the English ladies who coveted them for their fidelity, industry and skill in the whole range of domestic arts from needlework to bringing up children. When the Emperor insisted on Mary's being brought to Spain for her education as provided in the marriage contract, the English ambassadors refused on the ground that 'as concerning the bring up of her, if he (Henry VIII) should seek a mistress for to frame her after the manner of Spain, and of whom she might take example of virtue, he should not find in all Christendom a more meet than she now hath, that is to say the Queen's grace her mother . . .'

But the Spanish influence did more than to inculcate virtue. It affected almost the whole of the child's programme of education. In that respect Catherine had little prejudice to overcome since Spain was in the fashion. Not with the lower classes, of course, but they scarcely mattered, nor with the artisans of the cities who hated all foreigners and things foreign as competitors for their livelihood. But to the middle and upper classes Spain was not only the first nation of Europe but the friendliest, for reasons alike of business and sentiment: the wool-markets of the Low Countries, upon which English commercial prosperity was founded, and the Burgundian alliance, the ancient expression of English hostility to France, both having been absorbed into the orbit of Spanish polity. Of this system of relationships Catherine's marriage, like that of her sister Joanna to the heir of Burgundy and the Netherlands, had been intended as the visible acknowledgement and pledge. As trade and politics drew the two countries together, affairs increasingly took Englishmen to Spain, whence they returned smitten with the fascination of Spanish culture. The writings of the great Spanish theologians began to be studied alongside those of the Italian classicists and profoundly to affect the thought of the wonderful group of writers and thinkers then at work in England—Colet, Linacre, Erasmus and More among others—trying to reconcile the old faith with the new learning. Spanish scholars came to lecture in the universities and mingle in the intellectual life of London. Amongst them was Juan Luis Vives, one of the most celebrated of living humanists, whom Wolsey, after meeting him in Bruges in 1521, invited to fill one of his six newly-founded lectureships at Oxford. There for three years from 1523 the Spaniard taught classical literature and law, spending his holidays either at Bruges or at the court, which Erasmus described as an academy full of men learned in all kinds of studies standing round the royal table when literary and philosophical subjects were discussed. A warm believer in higher learning for women, Vives in the year of his arrival in England composed what was to become a classic on the subject, *De Institutione Feminae Christianae*, which he dedicated to Catherine, who thereupon appealed to him for advice on the schooling of her daughter. He responded with a Plan for Studies for Girls, *De Ratione Studii Puerilis Epistolae Duae*, also dedicated to Catherine. Not long afterwards he was given the general supervision of Mary's education.

His writings prove him to have been, even more than Erasmus or More, a pioneer—as his country was the pioneer amongst nations—in the sixteenth century movement for the higher education of women. But if he believed in improving them, he did not believe in pampering them. Improbably high as he set his bookish standards, his discipline was even more alarming: after reading the *De Institutione* his friend and admirer Erasmus expressed the hope that he did not treat his own wife like that. Though he does not specifically advocate the rod, he seems strongly to suggest that no responsible husband and father would shrink from using it where necessary in order to prevent his womenfolk from addling their brains with the romances then in vogue—those '*libri pestiferi*' like the Amadis de Gaul series and the other spiced and sugared confections of a putrescent chivalry for which the comic genius of a yet greater Spaniard was to supply the disinfectant. If reading for recreation was now and then required—and Vives did not exclude this craving in its proper place—there were the stories of Lucrèce and of Joseph, both of which he strongly, and rightly, recommended for their power to edify as well as to entertain. Moreover one came from the classics and the other from the Bible, the two cornerstones of his monumental programme. This directed his

pupil to read, morning and evening, a passage from
the New Testament or selected portions of the Old
together with extracts from one or other of a half-dozen
early Christian poets whose names would now mean
nothing except to specialists. Each day her Latin and
Greek grammar and pronunciation were to be perfected
by written and oral exercise, and her memory trained
by means of couplets, epigrams and similar mnemonics,
either in the original or in English translations, taken
from the classical sages and learned by heart. That this
should not become mere parrot's work Vives enjoined
the use of a good Latin-English dictionary, with the
caution that his pupil should ignore the obscene and
impolite words, though how the rule was to be enforced
he neglected to make clear. Regular informal conversation in Latin followed; to add the stimulus of variety
and competition, two or three girls of Mary's age were
added to the class on Vives' recommendation.

Thus prepared, the little group went on to confront the
syllabus of reading formulated out of his vast knowledge
and experience. To the modern eye it seems extraordinarily
narrow, reducible almost to the two headings of theology
and history without any very close distinction between
them. Into the one category ostensibly fell the selected
writings of the early Fathers, notably Saint Cyprian and
Saint Ambrose, the *Epistles* of Saint Jerome—chastity
further justified—and the *City of God* of Saint Augustine
though not the *Confessions*. Even here the stress seems
to be at least as great on history as on doctrine, on politics
as on apologetics, and the same emphasis is visible in the
prominence given to pagan writers like Cicero, Seneca,
Plutarch and Plato, from whose Dialogues those of a
political character are singled out. Among contemporaries
Erasmus—again largely for the political aspect of both
his editions of the classics and his original work—and the

Utopia of Sir Thomas More, published the year Mary was born, alone receive special notice.

What is omitted is almost as interesting as what is included. There is no mention of Saint Thomas Aquinas, the central figure in Catholic theology since late Roman times, whose teaching one would have thought indispensable to the rounded system of Christian thought which Vives had before him in forming the minds of his young charges. But the Spaniard, along with his fellow-humanists, had declared war upon the Scholastics whose futilities for over a century and more past had provoked the bitter mirth of the enlightened and not a little of the reaction which sped the Reformation; and their master Aquinas, who had elevated Aristotle to the primacy among philosophers in the thirteenth century, was tainted with their folly in the eyes of the sixteenth, for whom Plato was as a god and Saint Augustine his apostle to the Christians. It is true that a translation of a prayer of Saint Thomas's which Mary made at the age of 11 survives in a missal which she gave away as a present, but this proves little except her ability to render a convenient piece of Latin prose into fluent English; not only the mind of the saint, but the whole cultural riches of the Middle Ages, remained an almost unopened book to her, and for this the great Spanish Humanist who assailed the Scholastics at Oxford and dedicated his edition of Saint Augustine to her father was in large part responsible.

Even more striking is the small part played in her studies by what is commonly called imaginative literature. So far as Vives' syllabus went, neither Homer nor Virgil nor the other great Greek or Latin poets except Horace and Lucan merited close consideration; nor any of the dramatists except Seneca, who curiously exercised a profounder influence upon the creative minds of the sixteenth century than perhaps any other tragedian of antiquity. It was not that Vives himself was indifferent to poetry, but he seemed to regard it as of minor importance in his scheme of female education; and so far as the love poets like Anacreon and Sappho are concerned, he appears after an involved argument in his *De Institutione* to lump them with the romancers as too dangerous for woman's discretion. Nor did he apparently set any higher value on the sciences which were beginning to excite his contemporaries, both those with a passion for letters and those whom they provided with a substitute for that passion.

Vives did not, of course, account for the whole of Mary's education. Her study of Latin began before he came to England, and there is reason to believe that it was planned by an equally illustrious scholar, Thomas Linacre, Founder of the College of Physicians and Surgeons; a long allegory in verse written by her chaplain after her accession declared that

> . . . Emonge her Instructours, before other far, Highely florischeinge in the latyne tonge, She had the famous Thomas Lynaker, Whois Rules for her remaynethe us emonge . . .

and in fact a Latin grammar survives which he dedicated to her. Under such preceptors her progress was so swift that at 9 she was reputed on good authority to have reached the proficiency to be expected of a girl of 12; and her application continued unbroken, so that when she was Queen her idiomatic command of it in conversation with learned foreigners was considered even in that time to be remarkable. Spanish she most probably learned from her mother or one of her mother's intimates, but apparently dropped it, for at her first encounter with her Spanish husband she could understand but not easily answer him in his own tongue. Something of the same sort perhaps happened with her Greek, to which there is almost no later reference, but Greek was then largely the preserve of the erudite, and even men like Erasmus and Colet did not master it—if that is not too strong a word even for them—until their maturity. French she began early, certainly well before her 'teens, and was always able to speak with ease; her Italian, on the other hand, she used with hesitancy, as if she had learned it too late or too superficially to be able to think in it. Outside literature and languages—and perhaps in instinctive recognition of their disproportionate part in her equipment—she seems to have devoted some of her leisure hours after she had left the schoolroom to the sciences and acquired at least a smattering of geography, mathematics and astronomy.

In addition there were her music and needlework, which do not fall into quite the same category, though much time and instruction were devoted to them. Both were labours of love: her carefully kept accounts, which reflect her delight in giving presents, show frequent sums spent on choice bits of material to be worked with affectionate care into book or table covers or articles of dress to be given at the appropriate seasons to her friends and the many children of all social strata to whom she stood godmother from an early age. But for music she had not only a love but a gift which, like Henry VIII's, was of something more than the ordinary amateur order. She had just passed her second birthday when, being brought to the Presence Chamber for the usual homage, she spied at a little distance in the crowd Fra Dionisio Memo, the organist of Saint Mark's in Venice, whom her father had recently invited to England to become his 'chief instrumentalist', and summoned him with the glad cry of 'Priest!' to come and play for her, repeating the cry till he heard and obeyed. Under him and the other foreign music-masters who succeeded him, she continued her studies until well into maturity, achieving a skill and a finish, according to all descriptions, beyond that of any other royal person in Europe on the virginals, the lute and the little portable organ known as the regal— those quaint instruments which tinkle so dreamily to the fancy from the coloured brightness of contemporary tapestry.

These embellishments upon Vives' programme were in no sense criticisms but intelligent additions to it dictated by his pupil's special circumstances and endowments. But in one respect it was sensibly modified, namely the mood in which it was carried out; at least there was little sign of the rigours which had incited Erasmus' quip. On the other hand there was little room in it for the close and tender intimacy which, according to the same authority, regulated Sir Thomas More's approach to the educational problem—'There is no man so loving with his children. He loves his old wife as if she were a young maid.' But Princesses were not, and probably could not be, brought up in that way, and there was real imaginative understanding in Henry and Catherine's attention, often from afar, to their daughter's progress. The instructions drawn up by the Privy Council when Mary was sent at the age of 9 to represent the Crown in the Marches of Wales directed that

'First, principally and above all other things, the Countess of Salisbury, being Lady Governess, shall according to the singular confidence that the King's highness hath in her, give most tender regard to all such things as concern the person of the said princess, her honourable education and training in all virtuous demeanour. That is to say, at due times to serve God, from whom all grace and goodness proceedeth. Semblably at seasons convenient to use moderate exercise for taking open air in gardens, sweet and wholesome places and walks, which may confer unto

her health, solace and comfort, as by the said Lady
Governess shall be thought most convenient. And
likewise to pass her time most season at her virginals,
or other instruments musical, so that the same be not
too much, and without fatigation or weariness to
intend to her learning of Latin tongue and French.
At other seasons to dance, and amongst the residue
to have good respect unto her diet, which is meet to
be pure, well prepared, dressed and served, with
comfortable, joyous and merry communication in all
honourable and virtuous manner, and likewise unto
the cleanliness and well-wearing of her garments and
apparel, both of her Chambers and body, so that
everything about her be pure, sweet, clean and wholesome, and as to so great a princess doth appertain,
and all corruptions, evil airs and things noisome and
unpleasant to be foreborne and eschewed.'

Despite his own more ascetic temper there is no reason
to suppose that Vives would have disapproved of these
instructions, since he approved of the More establishment
as highly as did Erasmus.

He had the less reason for disapproving in that his
scheme, however modified in detail, remained unaltered
in its central purpose. It was not merely—in fact it was
far from—a plan for educating women in general, but
for forming, as its title declared, *Christian* women. The
distinction is vital. Erasmus, continuing his description
of More's family life, tells his correspondent, 'You would
say that his house was Plato's Academy. I should rather
call it a school, or a university, of the Christian religion.'
It is the same distinction repeated in other words. In the
view of Erasmus, as of Vives, Plato was taught that he
might serve Christ; in that respect there was no difference
between them and Saint Thomas or Saint Augustine.
To such teachers any doctrine of education for education's

sake would have seemed sheer nonsense. Since they were agreed that the end of man was to glorify God, the purpose of education could only be to articulate for the educated what every Christian was supposed to apprehend intuitively, namely that all things capable of being known were but so many evidences for the one ultimate truth already contained in God's revelation of Himself. These evidences might be added to from time to time and the interpretation placed upon them vary from age to age; it was the duty of men, especially of educated men, to weigh the new and reassess the old according to their best powers, even if it meant doing what the great Schoolmen had done, suspend all the evidences and re-examine in the light of pure reason the hypothesis that God did not in fact exist; experience as well as faith taught that every honest striving after knowledge, whether of the mind directly or empirically through nature, could not fail to add its quota to the existing proof of God's being and greatness. For the humanists such proof had been afforded through the rediscovery, in texts which scientific scholarship could respect, of a pagan wisdom so old that it had become new, and they in turn deemed it their task to articulate that wisdom with the 'true light which lighteth every man that cometh into this world'. This was the intellectual tradition in which Mary was reared. It explains Vives' choice of books for her studies, and why he could not sunder history and religion since history was primarily the evidence of God's activity in time.

Yet, however dominant the religious motive, it could not be allowed to exclude other motives from Mary's education. Time, in addition to being an aspect of eternity, had its own independent value, fully acknowledged by orthodox Catholic doctrine in allowing full reality to the world of sense—a very heightened reality in that particular time. For that world one called to such high place in it as Mary obviously required additional preparation neither intrinsically Christian nor even specifically feminine. Vives himself appeared to recognise this difference between her and the generality of women, since in laying down his plan for her studies he ignored his own principle stated in another work: 'as for the knowledge of grammar, logic, histories, the rule of government of the commonwealth and the art mathematical, they shall leave it unto men.' Mary's secular studies thus appear as appurtenances of her rank and function rather than of her sex; few women, and comparatively few men, would have had occasion to pursue and fewer still to use them. But for one destined possibly to inherit and at the least to share a throne, as indeed for all born or called to the business of ruling, they were indispensable to the understanding of the art of government as practised in different times and places and to dealing intelligently with the ministers of her own and other states. Hence this part of her instruction was carried out in what might almost be described as a utilitarian spirit. The practical took precedence over the imponderable, the *Republic* over the *Phaedrus*, the rebellious projects of Catiline over the rebellious passion of Antigone. What emerged was a set of principles out of the past deemed to have useful application in the present.

But at the same time something had been done to the past that strangely distorted its character. Seen in the hard light in which it was presented to Mary after the diffraction of its poetry and its mysticism, it tended to appear grandiose, didactic and conventional. With the individual and the unaccountable stripped away, heroism easily became confused with heroics and the infinite possibilities of human conduct reducible to a series of formal attitudes. Much that is characteristic of the century may be traced to this model on which it formed itself. The celebrated speeches from the scaffold, whether literally spoken or (as often happened) posthumously given the form in which it was felt that they ought to have been spoken, betray the inspiration of Plutarch and Seneca rather than the spontaneous agony of men and women faced with the last and most terrible of mortal facts. It was not in the canons of the Church or even in the Bible that Henry VIII found his most persuasive justification for divorcing Catherine but in the pagan doctrine that mechanical punishment followed upon unwitting sin: his marriage having proved sterile it must have been incestuous though contracted in good faith. Possibly Mary, too, was not unaffected by the lack of certain evident sensibilities in her education. The attempt to codify the past too readily tends to encourage the hope of giving rigidity to the future . . . a hope which underlies so much persecution.

CHAPTER TWO

The King's Secret Matter

The sons so confidently expected after Mary's birth had not followed. Their failure posed a problem which had not confronted England for 400 years. The objections to the obvious solution, namely, to take what was available, were grave, but it was the one that the King and his ministers appeared to have in mind in when in July, 1525, they decided 'to send at this time our dearest, best-beloved and only daughter . . . accompanied and established with an honourable, sad, discreet and expert council, to reside and remain in the Marches of Wales and the parties thereabouts.' Wales had a particular interest for the Tudors as the land of their origin. Remote and as yet largely unassimilated—Shakespeare in *Henry IV*, part I, was merely being funny with the truth—it was one of the hardest parts of the realm to govern. Henry VII had addressed himself to the difficulty by making it a sort of special appanage of the heir apparent and sending Prince Arthur to represent him on its borders after vesting him with the title of Prince of Wales. Henry VIII, in sending Mary in a similar capacity, thus appeared to acknowledge her in fact if not in form as Princess of Wales in her own right. As deputy of the Crown she personified the order and justice which had suffered from the King's long absence and which it was the mission of the accompanying council to restore and administer. In personal attendance upon her was a household headed by the Countess of Salisbury, her Lady Governess, with thirteen other ladies of high rank, a

Dean of the Chapel with two chaplains, a personal physician and an apothecary, a schoolmaster, a herald, a poursuivant, a cofferer, a clerk of the closet—a total of 304 persons altogether. New liveries were made in Mary's colours, blue and green, and towards the end of August the cavalcade set out for Thornbury in Gloucestershire. For most of the next two years, except for occasional visits to her parents, Mary moved about the West Country, keeping her principal headquarters at Ludlow where her mother had been left a young widow twenty-three years before.

In the same month that the King in Council decreed Mary's new establishment another of practically equal importance was awarded to her half-brother the Duke of Richmond. The two acts were not unrelated; taken together they reflect the confused anxiety of the King and his advisers. His only legitimate child was a girl; only once in English history had a female ruler succeeded, Matilda, daughter of Henry I, and the experiment had ended in civil war and the collapse of a dynasty. If the legal argument favoured Mary, considerations of policy told as strongly against her. Being a woman she would be expected to marry lest the dynasty perish; if she married a foreigner she might deliver her realm into the power of her husband's, if an Englishman, only too easily provoke a war of factions like that of the Roses, a fearful and vivid memory to people still in their prime, or like that of Stephen against Matilda. Nor was the legal argument itself without obscurities. The single precedent, quite apart from its disastrous consequences, had never amounted to a final settlement of the principle of female inheritance: the founder of the Tudor dynasty himself, Henry VII, had tacitly set it aside when assuming the Crown by virtue of a claim derived from his mother who was still alive. Parliament had made the law right in his case, as it had in others when the Crown passed by

violence. Though Henry VIII did not yet meditate
violence, he had some such hope of the law when he
raised his illegitimate son to outward parity of status
with his lawful daughter. The first step was to array
him in title and estate like a prince of the blood in order
that the country should become familiar with him in that
rôle, the next to induce Parliament to legitimise him and
then fix the succession upon him by formal act. Second
thoughts, however, suggested the danger that even if
Parliament could be brought to agree, the country might
not, and the very strife which Henry was seeking to
avoid be precipitated on his death between Mary's partisans and the Duke's. For a while he went so far as to
play with the idea of marrying the two and having them
proclaimed his heirs jointly. But the legalisation of incest
transcended the authority of Parliament and demanded,
if it did not exceed, the dispensing power of the Pope.
Henry decided not to put the matter to the test but to
proceed with another solution, both more appealing and
on the face of it less objectionable, which had in the meanwhile occurred to him.

In part this solution was not a new one. Some twelve
years earlier, in a mood of irritation at an artful trick
worked on him by Catherine's father, he had considered
having his marriage annulled because of her childlessness.
Being no more than a notion he allowed it to pass without
taking action: Henry was anything but impulsive in
spite of the deceptive antics to which his vanity or his
liberality sometimes prompted him. Mary's birth, which
coincided closely with the death of his father-in-law,
eased the situation with the expectation of the sons to
follow, until Catherine was 40 and had ceased having
even miscarriages. It was then that the various projects
took shape involving Mary and Richmond and the two
together. Henry sent Mary to Wales as Princess and soon
afterwards offered her to Francis I as heir-presumptive,

though other opinions held that he was trying to get rid
of her abroad in order to make way for her half-brother.
Francis I certainly took the former view, since it was in
the course of this negotiation that the French King's
delegate, the Bishop of Tarbes, interposed his shattering
query whether Henry, in putting Mary forward as his
heiress, was not ignoring the possibility that his marriage
was invalid and the girl therefore born out of wedlock.
It was to this remark that Henry later attributed the
decision at which he now arrived. His statement is true
only in part: at the most the Bishop could only have
crystallised doubts which Henry had heard and himself
expressed long before. But to focus attention upon the
juristic aspect of the matter helped to distract it from the
other, more personal incentive, which he preferred to
conceal, possibly even from himself. Never once did he
admit that Anne Boleyn was a contributory cause of his
divorce proceedings even after it became certain that she
was to be their first result. Even his closest confidant and
chief agent, the minister of whom a contemporary
historian wrote, 'all thyng that was doen was doen by
hym, and without his assent nothyng was doen'—echo
of another writer on a grander theme—even Wolsey
failed to suspect until it was too late that what he did to
rid Henry of Catherine he was doing on behalf of the
sprightly dark girl with the large demure mouth and
ambiguous black eyes to whom his master was writing
impassioned letters of desire and supplication.

She had returned from France, at whose court she
had passed most of her girlhood, a few years earlier owing
to a worsening of relations with that country at the time
of Mary's betrothal to the Emperor. Her connections
were excellent, including on her mother's side the Dukes
of Norfolk, and her attractions, though some flatly
denied them, were obviously considerable for others,
since the poet Thomas Wyatt fell in love with her and

the Earl of Northumberland, the most eligible bachelor of the moment, proposed for her hand and was accepted. Then Henry, who had formerly been her sister's lover, met her, caused the engagement with the Earl to be broken and took his own resolution to marry her. The wrong to her fiancé and the even deeper wrong to the wife whose husband's attentions she was accepting seem in no way to have troubled her: a callousness for which Henry, whose conscience was by no means equally easy, would one day call her to account. For Henry was genuinely concerned at the injury he meant to inflict on Catherine, though far from foreseeing how terrible it would be. Had he been able to marry Anne while remaining married to Catherine he would have been strongly tempted—in fact he at one time put forward that very proposal, only to change his mind before it could receive the Pope's sympathetic consideration. However it may have been on Anne's side, it was certainly not true on his that only her tantalising prudery goaded him into proposing marriage. Had he merely wanted to possess her, he did in fact succeed in possessing her before he married her, only to hurry on the marriage faster when he learned that she was pregnant so that her child might be born legitimate. That was the dominating consideration, to which Catherine, Mary, Anne and Anne's disappointing daughter were all subordinate. For the dynasty to be secure he must have a son and that son an unimpeachable title. It was this necessity that inspired the bizarre expedients with which he had toyed in regard to the Duke of Richmond and caused him to withdraw as useless, because legally dubious, his application for a licence to have two wives at the same time. It not only drove him to hasten his wedding with Anne before her child's sex could be known, but to deal with her more harshly even than with Catherine when she failed to bear him a son: for though he humanly confounded his passion for her with his wish for an heir, the wish persisted after the passion died and she with it.

Some time between New Year's Day, 1527, when the accounts for Mary's household on the borders end, and 23rd April, St. George's Day, she was brought to court for her betrothal to Francis I. She made little speeches of welcome to the French delegates in their own tongue and in Latin, wrote a composition for them in her clear, unaffected hand and entertained them with a performance on the virginals. The Bishop of Tarbes delivered an oration appropriate to the union of an heiress-presumptive of England with a King of France. The company then divided for dinner, which the Bishop and his colleague the Marquess Turenne as a special honour took privately with the King. Afterwards all met in the Queen's apartments, where Mary danced with the Marquess, who paid her many compliments which he later confirmed in a letter reporting her to be uncommonly pretty and intelligent but so undersized for her 11 years that she seemed unlikely to be ready for marriage until she was 14. The usual round of jousts, dances and theatricals followed, leading up to the grand farewell entertainment. This took place in the great gallery, at one end of which had been erected a stage concealed by a painted curtain which, at the appointed moment, was let down to reveal

'. . . a most verdant cave approached by four steps, each side being guarded by four of the chief gentlemen of the court, clad in tissue doublets and tall plumes, each of whom carried a torch. Well grouped within the cave were eight damsels of such rare beauty as to be supposed goddesses rather than human beings . . . arrayed in cloth of gold, their hair gathered into a net, with a very richly jewelled garland surmounted by a velvet cap, the hanging sleeves of their surcoats being so long that they well-nigh touched the ground, and so well and richly wrought as to be no small ornament to their beauty. They descended gracefully from their seats to the sound of the trumpets, the first of them being the Princess, with the Marchioness of Exeter. Her beauty in this array produced such an effect on everybody that all other marvellous sights previously witnessed were forgotten . . . On her person were so many precious stones that their splendour and radiance dazzled the sight, in such wise as to make one believe that she was decked with all the gems of the eighth sphere. Dancing thus, they presented themselves to the King, their dance being very delightful by reason of its variety, as they formed certain groups and figures most pleasing to the sight. Their dance finished, they ranged themselves on one side, and in like order the eight youths, leaving their torches, came down from the cave, and after performing their dances, each one took by the hand one of those beautiful nymphs, and having led a courant together, for a while returned to their places. Six masks then entered . . . in cloth of gold and silver. . . . They chose such ladies as they pleased and commenced various dances, which being ended the King appeared. The French Ambassador, the Marquess of Turenne, was at his side, and behind him four couples of noblemen, all masked and all wearing black velvet slippers on their feet, this being done lest the King should be distinguished from the others, as from the hurt which he lately received playing at tennis, he wears a black velvet slipper. . . . All were clad in tissue doublets, over which was a long and ample gown of black satin, with hoods of the same material, and on their heads caps of tawny velvet. They then took by the hand an equal number of ladies, dancing with great glee, and at the end of the dance unmasked, whereupon the

Princess with her companions again descended and
came to the King . . .'

who then whipped off her cap to exhibit her hair. Never
had Henry shown greater pride in her or striven harder
to set her off to the best advantage. A few days later the
Frenchmen left. Scarcely were they out of the country
than Henry had himself privately cited by Wolsey
before a legatine court on the charge of cohabiting with
a woman not his lawful wife.

Of this opening move in the suit that was to devastate
her life Mary almost certainly knew nothing; it is doubtful even whether Catherine did, though she already
suspected something of the sort. Outwardly both went
on pretty much as before. Wolsey departed for France
to enlist the interest of Francis I with the prospect—
unbeknown to Henry—of Henry's subsequent marriage
to a French princess; Henry's secretary quietly slipped
away to Rome to conclude an amicable arrangement with
the Pope—unbeknown to Wolsey—for freeing Henry
so that he might marry Anne. All this took up a long time.
Meanwhile Henry continued to share bed and board
with Catherine and she to see to his wardrobe and the
other housewifely comforts upon which in the course
of eighteen years he had grown to depend. Like many
sensual, self-willed men, he was at heart domestic: a
man to whom it was no less natural to drop in for a chat
with his wife after dinner—or in later life to sprawl at
his ease with his ulcered leg on his last wife's lap—than
to dismantle a whole social order because it would not
give him what he wanted. The family gatherings continued to be held at the usual seasons despite his growing
preoccupation with his divorce and his mistress. From
Christmas to Twelfth Night the royal household,
oblivious or temporarily forgetful of the impending
cataclysm, gathered to hear the repertory of songs care-

fully rehearsed for it by a collegiate choir, to see the boar's head brought in gilded and artfully decorated, and to shriek like children together over the frolics devised by the year's Lord of Misrule—frolics requiring a cast and properties as elaborate as those indicated in one lord's itemised expense account:

'two tabards, a man who played the Friar, another who played the Shipman, a stock of visors, coat-armour, hats, gold-foil, coney-skins and tails for the mummers, four dozen of clattering staves and two dozen of morice pikes, twelve crossbows, gunpowder and four gunners, frankincense, ten dozen of bells and nine morice coats, a hobby horse, straw to cover twelve men in a disguising and a man to kill a calf behind a cloth.'

On New Year's Day came the interchange of presents, graded according to the rank of the receiver as well as the love which the giver bore him; on Mary there still poured in articles like tall gilt cups overflowing with money from her father, a golden goblet or 'salt' from her godfather the Cardinal, gold pomanders (that so necessary protection against foul air), gold spoons—gifts which Mary not only repaid in proportion to her means, sometimes with the work of her hands, but further acknowledged with generous tips to the servants who brought them. The first positive notification of what was in store for her was the abrupt cessation of these presents the New Year following her father's separation from her mother, four years after the divorce proceedings had been started.

She would have known long before, of course, what was afoot even if she was never informed directly. She could hardly have failed to notice something in her mother's manner and expression, nor the disapproval expressed in the withdrawal abroad of Vives, to whom Catherine, a few months after the collusive hearing before Wolsey, 'wept over her fate that the man she loved more than herself should be so alienated from her as to think of marrying another.' Within a year 'the King's secret matter' had become the talk of Europe, and obviously impossible to keep from the ears of a child surrounded by so many people from all walks of life—courtiers and servants passing back and forth between her perambulating residence and the capital, doctors, priests, teachers and the many women to whom, in her frequent rôle of godmother, she stood in the precise relationship of 'gossip'. What she thought and felt can only be imagined. But the imagination must be on its guard against conceiving her thoughts and feelings in terms of her mere 11 or 12 years. Children developed rapidly amongst the upper classes in the sixteenth century; boys were made ready for the university at 14, girls for marriage sometimes even younger. The forcing process was applied with particular intensity to royal children, both because of the greatness of the responsibilities that awaited and the corresponding sense of fatality that overhung them. Henry VII, Henry VIII, Charles V and Francis I all died in their early or middle fifties, Mary's contemporary and one time fiancé Henry II of France at 40; of the sons who succeeded them only two were in their twenties, one was 18, one 14 and two were 9 years of age. In judging the acts of sixteenth-century kings that sense of fatality cannot be overlooked, nor its contribution to the precocity of their children. The process is written upon the portraits of the little princes and princesses, so staid and composed in their miniature replicas of their elders' clothes, their round childish faces stamped with sad suspicion and perplexed knowledge of many things they must not talk about.

At the end of May, 1529, just two years after the private hearing before Wolsey, the formal trial opened at Blackfriars Hall in London. Sitting with Wolsey as judge was the Pope's special legate Cardinal Campeggio, titular Bishop of Salisbury. The object, so far as Wolsey was concerned, was to obtain a verdict to the effect that Pope Julius II had exceeded his powers in granting a dispensation contrary to the Levitical injunction against marrying a deceased brother's wife and that the union of Henry and Catherine had therefore been illicit from the beginning—a verdict then to be rendered final and binding, upon pain of ecclesiastical censure upon any one who questioned it, by Pope Clement VII's confirmation. It was a squalidly dishonest performance, redeemed only by Catherine's tragic plea against the court's competence and Henry's almost equally moving tribute to her as wife and Queen. On the King's side the evidence for the consummation of Catherine's marriage with Arthur—a material point—consisted largely of the repetition at third hand of an adolescent's lascivious boast the morning after his nuptials: a species of testimony whose worthlessness was emphasised by the omission, certainly not out of squeamishness, to produce any witness to the obvious corollary. But Catherine, in refusing the Court's jurisdiction, was also on questionable ground. Though doubtless right in her belief that an impartial trial of the case was impossible in England, to press for its removal to Rome was so naive as to seem disingenuous. In May 1527, the month of Wolsey's first summons to Henry, the Emperor's mutinous troops had broken into the city, and driven the Pope into exile while they looted, burned, raped and murdered until brought to a halt by heat, plague and their own exhaustion. The Pope, living in terror of a repetition, was presently allowed to return as the Emperor's ostensible ally and actual dependent. A condition of the alliance, so basic that it hardly had need to be stated, was that nothing should be done to the detriment of the aunt or the cousin by whom the Emperor hoped to maintain and one day greatly to increase Spanish influence in England. The papal instructions to Cardinal Campeggio when he was sent to join Wolsey as Legate for the trial directed him to delay matters as long as possible and in no event to proceed to a verdict. If one judge was determined to give sentence beforehand against Catherine, the other was bound, whatever the facts, not to give it in favour of Henry: and on whichever side justice lay, it was not justice but the Emperor who prevailed when on the conclusion of the hearing in July the court was simply adjourned and the whole cause removed to Rome.

But power was a game at which two could play. While not yet despairing of having his way at Rome, Henry prepared to force Rome's hand if necessary by all and any means. That autumn his resolution claimed the first, most resplendent and perhaps the luckiest of its victims in Wolsey, who for his failure was deprived of his offices and most of his Arabian Nights' wealth and sent to rusticate in his archdiocese of York: whence he was summoned the following year to London to give an account of himself only to cheat the headsman of a fee by dying on the way. A fortnight after his dismissal the Parliament met which was to continue in being until it had solved the riddle of the divorce by setting up Henry as his own Pope endowed with the whole wealth and spiritual authority of the Church and the uttermost terrors of the secular arm with which to justify the solution against any who found it unsatisfactory. The mouse was to labour for over six years before it finally brought forth this mountain, but already in the early stages it became evident that Henry was changing. A lifetime of spoiling had left him unprepared for the resistance he was encountering over a matter in which he was so convinced of his own righteousness that, as he said, an angel straight from heaven could not have persuaded him otherwise. Moreover there was Anne, for whom his thwarted craving grew sharper while her reproaches grew shriller as the months passed and her anxiety mounted at the continuing favour shown to Catherine and Mary; and behind Anne was her family, inciting her in the immemorial fashion of the relatives of royal favourites, first against their common enemy Wolsey and then against the two principal obstacles to the crowning of her ambition. She worked for them and they for her. Well over a year before Wolsey's fall she had her father and brother in high office close to the King's person; shortly thereafter he was prevailed upon to install her openly at court.

The closer association mingled and inflamed their two angers against Catherine's obstinacy which alone prevented the consummation of their respective desires. On Catherine's side outraged dignity and Henry's increasing neglect also produced a deterioration of temper. For the first time they fell to open bickering. Shortly after the assembly of Parliament she demanded to know what she had done that he should treat her with such painful contempt. Henry retorted that she had nothing to complain of, being still Queen and well able to take advantage of the fact. The argument spun itself out, the dreary dialectic of the divorce was soon dragged in, authorities cited, hairs split and taunts exchanged, until Henry took himself off to Anne, who shrewdly observed that in any wrangle with his wife on that topic he was bound to get the worst of it. Her own tactics were to keep the two as much apart as possible and break down Catherine's resistance with ill-treatment and threats until she came to realise the hopelessness of her position. When Wolsey's fall left his London residence, York Place, vacant she persuaded Henry to spend long periods there because it was too small to include Catherine's household. At the same time she caused Mary's visits to her mother to be reduced in length and spaced at wider intervals.

But Catherine hung grimly on. To Henry's conviction of righteousness and the force of his desire she opposed her pride and her faith. Her father and her father-in-law, two wise and pious kings—for so she sincerely regarded them—had under God and with the Pope's approval chosen her as the instrument to unite Spain and England for the good of Christendom; she had done her duty and committed no fault; it was therefore inconceivable that God would permit her and her child to be deprived of their natural rights and cast out with the brand of concubine and bastard upon them. She would make no concession because she could not see that there was any concession possible—an attitude infuriating to Henry, who honestly believed that he was being patient and reasonable. At times when her heart grew faint with the struggle she seems to have been tempted to abandon it so far as she herself was concerned if only Mary's rights could be preserved; to a suggestion from Cardinal Campeggio that she might retire into a religious order she countered with an offer to consider it if Henry would do the same—a proposal which, had it come to anything, would have established Mary's position at once and for good. But Henry had no mind for the contemplative life and agreed only on the condition that the Pope would promptly release him from his vows while keeping his wife to hers. Possibly one of the more hurtful truths that dawned on Catherine at this period was that her husband was no longer to be trusted, with the result that the more he wished her out of his sight, the less did she dare to oblige him.

Mary fell ill, not once but several times; the period of her puberty was exceptionally difficult owing to the irregularity of function that was to torment her all her life, and with disastrous effect upon it. The doctors bled her often and expensively with small result until, out of her weakness and depression, she sent a plea to her parents that to be with them was the one medicine she needed. Instigated by Anne, who dreaded her lover's tenderness for his daughter more than any lingering sentiment for his wife, Henry refused. Catherine yearned to go to her, but feared to, with good reason. Henry himself brought the matter up again a few days later with a taunt to Catherine 'of her cruelty in that she had not had her own physician in constant attendance upon the Princess', into whose praises he then burst. Taking courage from this eulogy, Catherine next day renewed her application for the girl to be brought to Greenwich. Henry turned on her 'harshly and told her she might go to see the Princess if she liked and stay there.' To this Catherine responded as best she could with the assurance that 'she would not leave him for her or anyone else in the world.' Henry relented to the extent of allowing Mary to be sent for when the court moved to Windsor for the summer. Shortly afterwards, in July 1531, he left with Anne for a hunting expedition from which he sent back word that Catherine should make no effort to join him. She again tried the effect of the soft answer in a message regretting that she had not been allowed to say good-bye to him. But it was precisely that good-bye which Henry wished to avoid. A summons to Rome to argue his case in person had thrown him into a fury which demanded an outlet more adequate than words. For an interval long enough to be noticeable her message remained unacknowledged: then came, coupled with an outpouring of abuse for this last insult to which she had exposed him, the peremptory command to remove Mary to Richmond and herself to the More, a run-down manor lately detached from St. Albans Abbey, before his return with Anne to Windsor.

They never met again. Presently she was removed from

the More to Ampthill, then to Buckden in Huntingdon-
shire and finally to Kimbolton Castle, always deeper
into the recesses of the eastern counties and always to
smaller and unhealthier quarters which in the end shrank
to one room in which she carried on the whole business
of life, never leaving it, even for exercise, except to go to
Mass: a single damp, gloomy, long untenanted chamber
in which she brooded, prayed, wept, 'wrought in needlework, costly and artificially' vestments for the Church,
wrote her letters, slept and ate the food which the elderly
unpaid remnant of her household prepared and tasted
on the spot for fear of the poison which they hardly dared
hope they could long keep from being somehow administered to her. Few from the outside world ever saw
her, chiefly emissaries sent by her husband to demand in
vain her consent to her own degradation, or to rifle her
papers and commandeer her remaining jewels for Anne's
adornment, and of these rare visitors few after seeing her
ever expected to see her again.

Yet as she faded physically out of life, her spiritual
presence seemed to become more formidable and per-
vasive, haunting the imagination of her contemporaries
like some unexorcisable ghost. In the English people,
for whom the ramifications of the divorce had been too
confusing to arouse violent partisanship one way or the
other, her tangible wrongs excited an anguished pity and
a dangerous impulse to action; the legal obscurities lifted,
the conflict hitherto waged on the remote political heights
descended to earth and became a personal drama with the
injured wife and mother and the King's presumptuous
harlot as the antagonists. Charles V, to whom his aunt
while in the world and free had addressed fruitless
petitions for help, found her sorrowful spectre so har-
rowing the hearts of his subjects that their clamour for a
crusade of redress nearly upset the troubled balance
between his conscience and his calculations: nearly

enough, at least, for Henry, despite all his courage and effrontery, to greet the news of her death with the glad outcry, 'God be praised, we are now free of all suspicion of war!' Even so he spoke too early for in the same year his people's resentment broke out in insurrection. But it was upon Mary that her mother's invisible influence made itself most effectively felt. She was 16 when she last saw Catherine in 1532, nearly 20 when Catherine died in January 1536. They were the four years which saw the ancient order of Church and State overturned and some of the ablest and best of Henry's subjects destroyed in his pursuit of the one primary object which could not be fully realised unless Mary made her capitulation to the terrible will which had accomplished all the rest. That she was to resist so long was due almost alone to the ghostly presence at Kimbolton.

CHAPTER THREE

Anne's Failure

Her resistance was not immediately called for. It was from his wife and the Pope, not from his daughter, that Henry required subscription to his theory of marriage. Doubtless Mary disagreed with him and doubtless he knew it, but he took no offence, accepting it as natural that she should grieve at the separation of her parents and her own separation from one of them. Her subscription would in any event have been of little practical use to him, and so far it was the practical result that interested Henry and not, as later, a blind unanimity of assent to the arguments by which he justified it. Even towards Catherine his conduct was inspired less by malice than by gusts of exasperation at her obstinacy. Once he had cleared her out of his house he offered to set her up in the dignified luxury of a widowed sister-in-law if she would accept the corresponding status—an offer which, though it implied the restoration of her daughter's company, she rejected with a slash of the pen across the proffered title of Princess Dowager and the declaration that she would rather beg her bread from door to door than abate one jot of her just claims. To such an answer only one response was possible, but the tightening of Catherine's persecution continued to be varied by spasms of respectful regret that she should be so blind to her own best interests.

Hurt and at times—though it seems hard to credit— clearly perplexed by her attitude, he gave Mary no occasion to fall into a similar one. He asked nothing of her, did nothing to her except what followed incidentally upon his differences with others; the loneliness and growing dread in which she passed from adolescence to young womanhood were, given the whole state of affairs, as much beyond his control as hers. As between themselves nothing was openly altered. They remained on the same affectionate footing as before, hunting together and exchanging their customary presents, such as an extra allowance of pocket-money from him and the proud gift from her of a buck killed by her own hand for his table. She still ruled a household of 162 persons with the Countess of Salisbury as Lady Governess. So far as her expectations, including her title of Princess went, he not only refrained from calling them into question but threatened to punish anyone who should venture to do so.

And yet, not many months after the rupture with Catherine, he parted from Mary. This second separation, unlike the first, was apparently without previous intention on Henry's part; until it actually occurred, there had been no hint of it in any act or expression on either side. At one moment, according to the only record of their last meeting for over four years, they were standing together in a field towards midsummer after a day of sport; the next he was looking wistfully after her as she left him at his command on the approach of two of Anne's familiars. The incident suggests that it was his mistress's nagging and spying rather than any fixed resolution that caused Henry, out of sheer boredom and irritation, to put off seeing the girl again, always perhaps meaning to, until he supplied himself with a real and self-sufficing motive for not doing so. It was another draft on Anne's credit for which she would one day be called to account.

Between her and Henry the situation was already, at times, noticeably strained. After disrupting his family and surviving several quite painful if somewhat eccentric attacks of conscience for her sake; after making her a marquess in her own right and supporting her on a scale that insanely taxed his resources, after elevating her relatives to offices and dignities well beyond the counsels of prudence, she still kept him fretting after the consummation for which he had been pleading for nearly six years. In her own way she was as obstinate as Catherine, with not dissimilar, though not yet such dangerous, effects on Henry's temper. Until he found the means to take her legally she would not consent to be taken at all. But the legal solution rested with the Pope, and until Catherine, the Emperor's aunt, consented, the Pope dared not even if he would. Ever since the meeting of Parliament in the autumn of 1529 Henry had been experimenting with devices to alter the Pope's mind and will. In 1530 he had sent out a commission to gather support for his thesis, by argument or purchase or both, from the Universities of Europe, only to find that the counter-activities of his opponents had so divided the learned Faculties as to render any useful consensus of opinion impossible. In the same and the two subsequent years he had with the aid of Parliament first deprived the English clergy and later the Pope himself of various lucrative powers and privileges; from a frightened Convocation he had extorted the title of Supreme Head of the Church of England together with a heavy fine for having once upon a time received, at his behest, Wolsey as the Pope's representative. Seldom had so much energy been so furiously misapplied. The arguments and injuries designed for the Pope had not only instituted, in its early phase they *were* the Reformation: the great work of which pious generations had dreamed, the renovation in the government and morals of the Church to which Erasmus had called him and Wolsey hoped to conduct him when he got round to it, Henry had at last taken in hand. But in so remarkably fulfilling the aspirations of

others, he had strikingly failed to satisfy his own. He
was still bound to Catherine, still denied possession of
Anne. The deadlock of wills was as complete as it had
been in the beginning.

It was Anne who at last broke it. Perhaps it was
inevitable that it should be. Catherine had her faith
and her pride to sustain her, the Pope his great office
and the support of Christendom—before which many
even now thought Henry would eventually have to give
way—but Anne had only Henry whose will she was
resisting. If he grew finally impatient with her, or turned
his favours elsewhere—indeed there was already talk of
a rival—she was lost. She made her decision; some time
early in 1533 she knew she was pregnant: and Henry,
after six years of effort to justify a theory, was driven to
decisive action by a fact. The matrimonial knot that
refused to be unpicked would have to be cut, as Wolsey
had foreseen from the start. In April Henry and Anne
were secretly married at Greenwich. In May the marriage
between Henry and Catherine was pronounced invalid
at a private hearing at Dunstable by the new Archbishop
of Canterbury, Thomas Cranmer, whose appointment
Henry had managed to secure, not without a certain
trickery, from the Pope in time. On June 1st Anne was
crowned.

Nothing was yet done about Mary. Taught by hard
experience, Henry was taking no chances with the succession until his new wife proved herself better capable
than her predecessor of bearing living issue. On 7th
September the visible though disappointing proof appeared in the form of a female infant, christened Elizabeth
after Henry's mother. On 2nd October Mary's chamberlain Lord Hussey, notified her that he had that morning
received a letter from the Comptroller of the King's
household, Sir William Paulet, ordering the dissolution
of her household, then at Beaulieu (otherwise known as

New Hall) in Essex, and her removal to her half-sister's, shortly to be installed at Hatfield.

Mary declined to believe it. 'In most humble wise,' she promptly wrote Henry

'I beseech your grace of your daily blessing. Please the same to be advertised that this morning my Chamberlain came and shewed me that he had received a letter from Sir William Paulet, Controller of your house: the effect whereof was, that I should with all diligence remove unto the Castle of Hertford (sic.). Whereupon I desired him to see the same letter, as concerning the leaving out of the name of Princess; forasmuch as I doubt not in your goodness, but that your Grace doth take me for his lawful daughter, born in true matrimony. Wherefore if I should agree to the contrary, I should in my conscience run into the displeasure of God, which I hope that assuredly your Grace would not that I should. And in all other things your Grace shall have me always as an humble and obedient daughter and handmaid, as ever was child to the father, which my duty bindeth me to, as knoweth our Lord who have your Grace in his most holy tuition, with much honour and long life to his pleasure.

By your most humble daughter
Marye Princess'

It was not the tone commonly adopted towards sixteenth-century monarchs, even on the part of indignant and incredulous 17-year-old daughters. But Mary was not disputing Henry's orders; she was questioning whether they *were* his orders. Right to the very end, long after it was possible to harbour any doubt on the subject and she had been brought to write letters as abject as any ever addressed by one human being to another, she still clung to the belief that her humiliations were the work of sinister forces surrounding her father and that if she could but once speak to him face to face they would instantly cease. Her unshakable faith in his love and justice is in a sense the key to all that follows.

Henry did his best to enlighten her. Without answering her letter directly—the policy he henceforth adopted with respect to all her communications—he sent the Earls of Oxford, Essex and Sussex, together with Dr. Sampson, the Dean of his Chapel, as spokesman, to convey to her 'and all other the officers and servants of her household' that

'The King is surprised to be informed both by Lord Hussey's letters, and by his said daughter's own, delivered by one of her servants, that she forgetting her filial duty and allegiance, attempts, in spite of the commandment given her by Lord Hussey, and by the letters of Sir Will Paulet, Controller of the Household, arrogantly to usurp the title of Princess, pretending to be heir-apparent, and encourages others to do the like declaring that she cannot in conscience think but she is the King's lawful daughter, born in true matrimony, and believes the King in his own conscience thinks the same. That to prevent her pernicious example spreading, they have been commanded to declare to her the folly and danger of her conduct, and how the King intends that she shall use herself henceforth, both as to her title and her household. That she has worthily deserved the King's high displeasure and punishment by law, but that on her conforming to his will he may incline of his fatherly pity to promote her welfare.'

The nature of the benefits towards which Henry's fatherly pity might incline him were indicated in a letter she received from her mother at about that time. As well as threatening Mary directly, Henry was threatening her through Catherine and, conversely and even more emphatically, Catherine through her in order to enlist the mother's influence on her child. That summer he had begun to intensify both his physical and moral persecution of his wife, and as part of the process had warned her 'that chiefly she should have regard to the Honourable and her most dear daughter, the Lady Princess; from whom, in case the King's highness, (being thus enforced, exagitated and moved by the unkindness of the Dowager) might also withdraw his princely estimation, goodness, zeal and affection, it would be to her no little regret, sorrow and extreme calamity.' Catherine, without fear for herself, refused to assist her husband by infecting her daughter with it. Soon the hint became more explicit: not only was Mary called upon to abandon her title and offer the assent which her mother withheld, but it began to be rumoured that she was to be forced or tempted into a nunnery or an unworthy marriage abroad. The rumour, reaching Catherine, drew from her the most revealing and in some ways touching of all her letters. Though without date or, most unusual for her, place, it must have been written between the withdrawal of the title of Princess from Mary at the beginning of October and the dismissal of the Countess of Salisbury late in December:

'Daughter, I have heard such tidings to-day that I do perceive, if it is true, the time is come that God Almighty will prove you; and I am very glad of it, for I trust he doth handle you with a very good love. I beseech you, agree to His pleasure with a merry heart; and be you sure that without fail He will not suffer you to perish if you beware to offend Him. I pray you, good daughter, to offer yourself to Him. If any pangs come to you, shrive yourself; first make you clean; take heed of His commandments, and keep

them as near as He will give you grace to do, for then
are you sure armed. And if this lady do come to you,
as it is spoken, if she do bring you a letter from the
King, I am sure, in the selfsame letter, you shall be
commanded what you shall do. Answer you with few
words, obeying the King your father in everything,
save that you will not offend God and lose your own
soul; and go no further with learning and disputation
in the matter. And wheresoever and in whatsoever
company you shall come, (obey) the King's commandments. Speak you few words, and meddle nothing. I
will send you two books in Latin: one shall be de
Vita Christi, with the declaration of the gospels, and
the other the Epistles of Hierome, that he did write
always to St. Paula and Eustochium; and in them I
trust you will see good things. And sometimes, for your
recreation, use your virginals, if you have any. But
one thing especially I desire you, for the love you
owe unto God, and unto me, to keep your heart with
a chaste mind, and your body from all ill and wanton
company, (not) thinking nor desiring any husband,
for Christ's passion: neither determine yourself to any
manner of living until this troublesome time be past,
for I dare make sure that you shall see a very good end,
and better than you can desire. I would God, good
daughter, that you did know with how good a heart
I do write this letter unto you. I never did one with
a better, for I perceive very well that God loveth you . . .
I beseech Him of His goodness to continue it; and if
it fortune that you shall have nobody to be with you of
your acquaintance, I think it best to keep your keys
yourself, for howsoever it is, so shall be done as shall
please them. And now you shall begin, and by likelihood I shall follow. I set not a rush by it; for when they
have done the uttermost they can, then I am sure of the
amendment. I pray you recommend me unto my good

Lady Salisbury, and pray her to have a good heart, for we never come to the Kingdom of Heaven but by troubles. Daughter, wheresoever you (be)come, take no pains to send for (to?) me, for if I may I will send to you.

> By your loving mother,
> Katharine, the Quene.'

The identity of 'this lady' and the character of the letter she was expected to bring cannot be more exactly determined, nor even whether such a person did in fact come bearing instructions from Henry in that way; possibly Catherine had heard that Anne's aunt, Lady Shelton, in whose charge Mary was to be placed, would be sent to take over from Lady Salisbury before the removal from Beaulieu. The phrase 'neither determine yourself to any manner of living' seems to refer to the hints going round that the girl was to be disposed of in a religious order, while the warning against fixing her thoughts on a husband almost certainly alludes to the efforts already in contemplation to direct her to that way of escape from her predicament. The caution 'to keep your keys yourself' clearly foresees the espionage and isolation in store for her. But more important than any concrete references in the letter is the insight it offers into Catherine's mind and the nature of her influence upon her child. Her vision of the world is wholly Christian, an austere and illuminated Christianity. Pain and evil are part of the mystery of its structure, but part also of the mystery of salvation, to be embraced and welcomed as such. Lesser authorities—a king's, a parent's—are respected as elements of the divine order, delegations of the supreme authority, but so also is the gift of reason given to man so as to enable him to discriminate between the supreme and the delegated. She is prepared to see her daughter suffer for the service of God—for the maintenance of the

CATHERINE OF ARAGON
British School

ANNO DNI · 1 5 4 ·

LADI MARI   DOVGHTER T
THE MOST   VERTVOVS PRIN
KINGE HENRI   THE EIGHT

THE AGE OF   XXVIII YER

MARY TUDOR
by Master John

Church He had founded and the basic rules He had laid
down for human conduct—but not to gain the satisfaction
of having said her say, put others smugly in the wrong,
aired her vanity in her own 'learning and disputation'.
But in all this there is also a danger, especially for a young
and enthusiastic person, which Catherine in her purity
may not have appreciated and even if she had, could not
in the circumstances, very well have stressed. Of all
perils to the deeply religious temperament, the most
insidious is the conscious even if humble assurance of
God's approval—of Providence having so organised
suffering as to allow the inference of election to be unmistakably drawn from it by the cheerful sufferer.
One wonders whether Catherine, so free of it herself,
already detected signs of this fateful trait in Mary.

In one detail Mary did not even now literally follow
her mother's advice. When the Duke of Norfolk appeared on Christmas Day to remove her, by force if
necessary, to 'the court and service' of Elizabeth, 'whom
he named Princess', she demurred hotly. The title belonged to her and no other; the position in which they
proposed to place her was strange and dishonourable.
There was no reply the Duke could make, but equally
nothing that the angry girl could do. Asking for half an
hour to make ready, she retired to her room and there
signed a 'protestation' to the effect that if she were constrained by force or fraud to renounce her rights, marry
by no choice of her own or enter a convent, she repudiated
any such acts to her prejudice in advance. Returning to
the Duke she implored him to ask the King that her
dismissed servants might be given a year's pay and then
asked how many she might bring with her. After discussion he granted her two, saying 'she would find an
abundance where she was going'. The old Countess of
Salisbury, her devoted companion since infancy, offered
to go along 'with an honourable train' at her own expense,

but the Countess was already under the suspicion which a few years later brought her to so terrible an end, and the Duke refused. Mary then entered her litter and set off for Hatfield. In the course of the journey the King's almoner, Dr. Fox, who had accompanied Norfolk, rode to the side of the litter and took the opportunity when unobserved to tell her that 'she had done well not to submit . . . and for the love of God besought her to remain firm.'

The authority for the foregoing scene is the young Burgundian lawyer, Eustace Chapuys, who since 1529 had represented the Emperor as Ambassador at the Court of St. James. A very large part of what is known in those years both of Mary and her mother is based upon his reports to Brussels of what he had himself observed or was able to gather from sympathetic informants and paid spies. He was Catherine's principal adviser and, except for Catherine, Mary's; it was he who had actually drafted the 'protestation' she left at Beaulieu. How far his testimony is trustworthy is a matter for individual discrimination. At times it can be weighed against other evidence, at times it stands alone and has to be assessed according to the uncertain standards of psychological probability. He venerated Catherine, had a profound, protective pity for Mary, despised Anne, distrusted but on the whole respected Henry. On the other hand he took very seriously his duty of transmitting as accurate a picture of the position to his master as possible, and his good-humoured shrewdness and ability to appreciate even when he did not share their point of view gained him considerable confidence from Henry and his ministers.

Moreover he by no means always saw eye to eye with Catherine, still less with Mary; though they trusted implicitly in his friendship, they sometimes strongly dissented from his advice. His loyalty, zeal and experience, though invaluable to them, belonged primarily to the Emperor: and what the Emperor required was a political negotiator without too many prejudices or scruples who would know how to bargain and compromise for him according to the needs of the moment. Even for Catherine, despite the almost complete identity of her feelings as well as her interests with her nephew's, the Ambassador's recommendations were at times hard to swallow; but to Mary, so much younger and less profoundly Spanish, so much surer of the rightness of her few simple ideas and still unschooled to the lessons of compromise and dissimulation, the lack of religious emphasis, the apparent indifference to spiritual fundamentals, could sometimes render his devices for her welfare downright unpalatable. Sometimes she questioned them, even when endorsed by Catherine, more than once rejected them. In the great drama provoked by her birth and moving towards the determination of her destiny she was at last at 17 a character in her own right—a tiny pink-and-white character with a deep mannish voice, a quick if rigid mind and a will fearless to follow where her conscience led.

With her two attendants she arrived at Hatfield, where she was placed in charge of Lady Shelton, Anne's maternal aunt. The Duke of Suffolk, former husband to the aunt for whom she was named, greeted her with the demand that she go and pay her respects to the Princess. She answered that she knew no princess in England except herself, and that the daughter of Madam de Pembroke (the marquisate awarded to Anne) had no such title; but that it was true that since the King her father acknowledged her to be his, she might call her 'sister' as she called the Duke of Richmond brother. As she was retiring Suffolk asked her what word he should carry to the King. 'None else,' she replied, 'except that his daughter the Princess begged his blessing,' and when the Duke protested 'very roughly' that he could not carry such a message, curtly bade him to leave it.

Henry gave Suffolk a scolding for his failure, saying he had gone about his errand 'too softly'. Yet to Chapuys and others he gave the impression of being as fond of Mary as ever, and, despite loud threats 'to abate her stubborness and pride' in fact took no further steps against her for a time. He had no need to; he had but to leave it to Anne and those dependent on her. The Concubine, as Chapuys nearly always called her, had openly sworn 'to break the haughtiness in this unbridled Spanish blood', and Henry could have no reason to suppose that she would stop at anything to fulfil that vow. She could reasonably reckon that Henry was unlikely ever to be reconciled to Catherine, who therefore constituted in her own person no danger to herself and might, in view of her health and the ill-treatment she was undergoing, be expected presently to die. But Mary was another matter. Unless she could be brought, publicly and in unequivocal terms, to confess herself debarred from the succession as a bastard, it remained within the bounds of possibility for Henry to take her back into favour and consign Anne and her clique to perdition. That this was what the English people yearned for even she could not doubt. The open dislike and derision which greeted Anne on her public appearances, the warm, outspoken, compassionate acclaim given Mary by the crowds that collected at every flying hint that she was to appear at a window or travelling along a road, were suggestions that Henry might well take into account should he once begin to calculate his gains against his waning popularity.

There were also other, more poignant motives of jealousy. If it galled Anne to hear Henry speak of his first wife with a nostalgic respect that was hardly flattering to the second, it terrified her to note how the tears still came suddenly into his eyes when Mary was praised in

his hearing and with how much more sadness than anger
he joined in condemning her disobedience. Deep in her
heart she could not but suspect that his love for his first-
born was more powerful and abiding than his by now
fitful passion for herself, and to policy was added a
malignant spite which drove her to seek from her cruelties
to her step-daughter satisfaction no less than security.

'I hear,' reported Chapuys, 'she has lately boasted
that she will make of the Princess a maid-of-honour in
her royal household, that she may perhaps give her too
much dinner on some occasion, or marry her to some
varlet, which would be an irreparable evil.' From Anne's
point of view either of these solutions would have been
perfect because they would have been final. But though it
was later alleged against her that she had actually tried to
poison Mary, and her own brother was understood to say
that she hoped that Henry would pay a proposed visit
to France without her so that she could deal with the girl
as she listed regardless of the consequences to herself,
the wish was probably stronger than the actual willingness
to risk discovery and Henry's consent to her trial for
murder. Nor without Henry's connivance was it possible
for her to contrive Mary's marriage as she would have
liked; and Henry, who that winter turned down Alessan-
dro dei Medici on the ground that a Florentine duke was
not good enough for the royal blood of England, was most
unlikely to prove agreeable to pairing his daughter with a
varlet.

But beyond this Anne was left free to work on her step-
daughter pretty much as she liked. Almost every hardship
that fear or spite could invent was inflicted upon her. Lest
the neighbouring populace should see and cheer her,
she was forbidden to walk for exercise in the garden or the
public gallery of the house, or to attend Mass at the
church which adjoined it, but kept closely confined to
her meagre quarters. Yet even a welcome privacy was

denied her, for the privilege first accorded her of being
served in her room before making her appearance at the
common table was taken away on orders from Anne, who
decreed that she should do her eating and drinking like
the rest without giving herself royal airs, or starve.
Meanness went so far as to grudge her the breakfast
prescribed by her physicians for her health on the ground
of added inconvenience and expense ('at the least to the
sum of £26.13.4' for three months) to Elizabeth's
household. Her rooms were searched and her private
papers removed for examination, her maid abruptly
dismissed, 'without any one to go to or means of supporting herself', on the suspicion of having smuggled in
letters from Catherine and Chapuys; her friend and former
attendant, Lady Hussey, was imprisoned in the Tower
and searchingly examined regarding a small gift from
Mary which she had acknowledged by letter, on a chance
encounter she had had with her, on two slips of the
tongue when out of old habit she had addressed her as
Princess. In the effort to cut Mary off from the world the
same rigorous espionage was applied to all of her friends,
especially the Countess of Salisbury and the related house
of Courtenay of which the Marquess of Exeter was the
head. But Mary's sympathisers were too many and too
well distributed through every class of society, and
Chapuys could always, though with increasing difficulty,
find means of passing a message, oral or written, through
Anne's cordon of watchers. In a fury of frustration Anne
sent a sharp rebuke to her aunt for her leniency to her
charge 'considering the bastard that she was' and ordered
her to try the effects of a few smacks across the face, but
this went too far even for that obedient placewoman, who
staved off the execution of the order with a plaintive
tribute to Mary's 'goodness and virtues'.

Not one concession, however, or even whimper could

her tormentors extort from her. When overcome with misery she might 'retire to weep in her chamber', as Chapuys reports her doing 'constantly', but in public she held her head high. On one occasion Anne, apparently uneasy at the ill-success of her policy, sent her an invitation to discuss things face to face: but the bearer brought the message as from the Queen, and Mary answered simply that she knew no queen in England but her mother. Another time, finding herself nearly destitute and compelled to ask the King for clothing or the money with which to buy it, she cautioned the gentlewoman who carried her request to accept no answer from which her title of Princess was omitted. At times her insistence on this point took forms that seem to approach the ridiculous. When Elizabeth's household left Hatfield for the More, Mary declined to make part of her suite, saying she would go before or after but not as one of her attendants on the road. So she had actually to be placed in her litter by force—an attitude on her part which even worried Chapuys lest it might needlessly provoke Henry. But the gesture seems to have been more impressive than provocative, for at the household's next removal she was given, instead of an inferior leather-covered litter, one covered in velvet like Elizabeth's. This time Chapuys warned her in advance to precipitate no scenes, so she made arrangement with the Comptroller of the Household to be excused from forming part of Elizabeth's train. The promise was broken, perhaps at the instigation of higher authority. Mary, coming to the door, found her own equipage drawn up behind her half-sister's; so, taking advantage of a permission to choose her place in the procession, she pushed forward with such determination as to arrive at Greenwich independently an hour in advance and secure 'the most honourable place' in the barge that was to carry the party on to Richmond. On a subsequent occasion she evaded the difficulty by going the whole way by water while Elizabeth went by road.

The points she thus scored were small, but they were not trivial in the eyes of an age that attached such vast importance to externals. Royalty was recognised by certain definite attributes of separateness, just as membership of the gentry was recognised by the right to display arms; deprivation in either case was equivalent to declassification. For Mary to refuse to appear in Elizabeth's train was as vital to the principle for which she and her mother were fighting and suffering as the more painful refusal of the suggestion conveyed to her that she might live with Catherine if she would 'be content not to be called Princess', lest those who now favoured her 'would cool towards her, not knowing the causes of her actions'. Once let any action of hers, no matter how apparently insignificant, permit a doubt as to who were the Queen and Princess, who the concubine and bastard, a confused and timorous public opinion would rapidly magnify the doubt into a conclusion.

Clear-headed in most other respects, the great illusion persisted that she had but to speak with her father for all to be well again. Often she must have been—sometimes her words almost affirm that she was—sorely puzzled that the mighty, splendid figure whose love for her had been as unmistakable as the awe of others for him should have allowed himself to be wheedled into permitting such things to be done to her. She never openly complained of him, and rarely to him, firm in the conviction that he had been misled into believing her an unfilial, disobedient daughter; others might tell her but, until he told her so himself, she could not really conceive it possible for him to question that her mother was his wife by divine sacrament and she his lawfully begotten child; and that being so, she could not terminate her status of Princess, even had she desired to do so in order to please him,

any more than she could alter her parentage or the
physical characteristics with which it had endowed her,
as he must surely see if he would but afford her an opportunity to explain.

The chance, the last chance, for that explanation
occurred shortly after her removal to Hatfield. Henry
paid a visit, ostensibly to his younger daughter but also,
it was confidently stated in court circles, drawn by a
longing to see and persuade his elder. Hard after him
rode several of his ministers, headed by the chief of them,
Thomas Cromwell, whom Anne had despatched to
prevent a meeting she dreaded as fervently as Mary
longed for it. Henry listened and yielded. He, too, had
reason to fear an interview whose outcome he could not
foresee. Aware of his variable moods towards his 'jewel of
the world', he could not but be uneasy in his own mind as
to what he might say or do. If he failed to persuade,
he might be driven to utter threats which he would be
reluctant to carry out; if nothing at all came of it the
impression on the public mind would be unfortunate
and he would needlessly have stirred up Anne. Instead of
seeing Mary he sent a message ordering her to accede
to his wishes. Without agreeing or refusing she returned
a request that she might be allowed to come and kiss his
hands. As he mounted his horse to depart she came out
on to a terrace at the top of the house to see him and he,
turning, caught sight of her on her knees with her hands
clasped as if in prayer. With an inclination of his head
he raised his hand to his hat in salute and his attendants,
closely watching, uncovered and 'bowed low'. The
chance had been missed, with incalculable consequences.
When they looked on each other again it would be no
exaggeration to say that they were two different persons,
so much had been done by him, so much done to her.

Already he had changed in a way and to a degree that
she, so long cut off from him, could not have suspected.

She had known him best in his ebullient, almost irres-
ponsible youth, when he had delighted to play the parts
of royal warrior, scholar and athlete in a manner somewhat suggestive of the brilliant amateur over-acting,
and leave Wolsey to do the work and shape the decisions
for him. Now, in his forties, too poor for wars, too preoccupied for scholarship and too fat and unwieldy for
athletics, he had discovered the even more satisfying
delights of power. It was not only that he now ruled
where he had once reigned, he had drastically revised the
very conception of ruling. The limitations upon arbitrary
individual power which his forbears and he himself
had so long assumed to be binding he had very largely
done away with; the claims of the Church and the tradi-
tional laws of the land, which they and he alike had
regarded as the supernatural and natural manifestations
respectively of the divine plan for human government,
he had exposed as mere figments without avail except
against fools prepared to be taken in by them. He did
not pose these innovations as theories—had they been
so presented to him he would in most cases have repudiated them—for he was not an original thinker but a man
of energy and appetite; he simply introduced them step
by step as circumstances required and permitted. The
Church was not radically altered, merely transferred
piecemeal to his control, the law was not openly flouted
but converted into an instrument of his will. Indeed,
thus far at least, the correct legal forms had been observed in subverting the old constitutional substance—a
process to be rendered monotonously familiar four
centuries later. A parliament representing a small minority
of the populace but composed of men whose interests
and ambitions in general coincided with Henry's gave
its approval, after more or less discussion, under pressure
skilfully proportioned to its scruples, to Bills laid before
it by an able chief minister for whom the immediate

evidences of power were the ultimate objects of reverence. So, early in 1534, was passed an Act of Succession which, in bastardising the King's first-born and giving to Parliament the disposal of the Succession, overturned the ancient principle of hereditary right, and later the same year an Act of Supremacy which codified Henry's pretensions to be Christ's vicar on earth so far as England was concerned.

These inter-related Acts were not mere informatory declarations; as well as ordering what the King's subjects might or might not do, even what they might or might not say, they laid down what they must think, with an oath of enforcement by which their thoughts might be tested, and penalties ranging to disembowelment if those thoughts proved sufficiently illicit to be construed into a menace to the King's peace of mind. The majority of those to whom the oath was submitted, though far from sharing the views of the select governmental majority, took it out of fear or apathy, but amongst those who refused were a number whose refusal most mattered. Against them Henry had now to institute a reign of terror unparalleled in English history. Into the seclusion of the Charterhouse penetrated his examiners and from it hauled to Tyburn the choicest living examples of an ancient spiritual discipline; to the Tower and presently the block went John Fisher, brightest ornament of the English priesthood, and after him Sir Thomas More, most illustrious of English laymen and once the most cherished of Henry's servants and friends; and after them followed others heedless of virtue, service or rank—including Catherine's chaplain Dr. Abell and Mary's tutor Dr. Featherstone—until the thing had become such a habit that the formalities of trial could be virtually stripped down to the essentials of arrest and condemnation.

Henry had at last encountered the limits of power. The

executioner's carving knife and axe were inadequate to compel all to think like the King or to say what they did not think. He could not stop himself because he had construed disagreement into treason, he could but go on doing the same thing over again, increasingly fearful that each dissent uncovered represented an unascertainable fraction of dissent still to be exposed. There was no longer room in him for gratitude, trust or affection; it proved impossible to exact fear from others without giving back what he received, nor did it escape the notice of shrewd observers that, however boastful, truculent and over-bearing he appeared, underneath he was 'wonderfully afraid'. Nevertheless he still fancied that he could when he chose carry off the part of the Merry Monarch, though it was like trying to dress his swollen body in the garments of his slender youth. Few were taken in, but they included, ironically, the discarded wife and daughter in whose memories he still was what he wished to appear, and who, thus remembering him, loved him for what he had once been.

In due course the officers of the law came to administer to each of them in turn the oath to the Act of Succession. They stood in greater peril than ever before and they knew it; their assent was incomparably more important than any cloistered monk's, or even Bishop's or ex-Lord Chancellor's. They refused, of course, more than once. On that ground they were prepared to stand or die. To the world at large it seemed quite likely that they would die; the officers who tendered the oath intimated as much, the supervisors set over and round them confidently and repeatedly predicted it in their hearing. Yet even this, if it were to come, they declined to impute to Henry. He was not himself, not acting of his own free will, he was bewitched by the woman to whom they sometimes alluded with less than Christian charity. (Though not much less: they never referred to her by

one of the synonyms for whore which the general public
freely employed, and now and then brought themselves
to pray for her.) And by bewitched they meant something
quite specific, some direct invocation of the powers of
evil. The notion was not peculiar to themselves. It was
held by many who had no particular use for Henry.
Chapuys registered his belief that 'this woman has so
perverted him that he does not seem the same man' and
spent much calculation on how she had done it, whether
by love philtres or private bargain with the devil. Henry
himself came in the end, when finally cured of Anne,
to favour this explanation of her spell over him.

Doubtless the mother and daughter exaggerated the
extent as well as mistaking the nature of their enemy's
power, but they in no way magnified her malevolence.
She, too, was fighting for her life now, against Mary
much more than Catherine. She could feel, even now
and then admitted, that her hold over Henry was slipping.
It had never been the deep, stable sort capable of maturing
into a proper husband-and-wife relationship but an
appeal to what was grossest in him, his lust and his
vulgarity. At a great dinner given in her honour after
their secret wedding but before its proclamation, Henry
shouted across the table to the old Duchess of Norfolk
to admire the gold and silver plate heaped on the side-
board, notoriously his gifts to the mistress he was at the
moment fondling in sight of the whole court, and demanded, 'had she not a great portion? And was she not a
goodly match?' He would not have asked the question
after a year had passed, and still less after another, when
the terror was adorning the more prominent vistas of his
capital with gory heads stuck on spikes and he, execrated
at home and abroad, continued to wait in vain for her to
produce the son who could alone make sense of his
proceedings. His craving no longer found its natural
compensation but had become an ambivalent fluctuation

between fierce desire and equally fierce loathing interspersed with livid bickering and hysterical reconciliations. He had other women now and, when she protested, curtly retorted that she would have to put up with it like her betters before her. With the irony of justice he had come to despise her for her part in their joint betrayal of Catherine. With equal irony Catherine had now become in one respect her best guarantee of safety. Henry would hardly dare to divorce her while Catherine lived lest by denouncing the validity of his second marriage he should seem to reinstate the first, the one having been justified by the same arguments which had been used to disallow the other. If on the other hand Catherine succumbed to her ailments and miseries, as was reported to be increasingly likely, and her daughter survived, not only the senior but obviously dearer to Henry than her own . . . the ominous possibilities opening before her seemed to come much closer when Henry, under the influence of a new mistress (never satisfactorily identified in the current references to her) showed an inclination to alleviate Mary's ill-treatment.

In her desperation Anne swung between two frantic extremes. At times no expedient seemed too bizarre if it would procure her step-daughter's death, at others none too humiliating if it might purchase her good-will. She declared herself ready to forfeit her own life to Henry's vengeance if she could but bring him to the mood to award her Mary's. With a kind of maniacal shrewdness she informed him of definite information granted her from supernatural sources—a curious confirmation of the belief that she was dabbling in the black arts—that she would never have male children while Mary lived. Then she would turn round and offer the girl a reconciliation with her father and such brilliance of position as she had never before enjoyed if she would accept the facts as the law declared them. Once, in the

spring of 1535, after both had left the chapel at Eltham,
where Elizabeth was in residence, word was brought
to Anne by one of her maids that 'the Lady Mary at
parting had made a reverence to her'. Anne eagerly
answered that she had not observed it but that 'if we had
seen it, we would have done as much to her' and sent a
lady of honour to bear her excuses and the assurance
that 'the Queen . . . desires that this may be an entrance
of friendly correspondence which your grace shall find
completely to be embraced on her part'. The message
reached Mary as she was sitting down to dinner. With
quiet sarcasm she pointed out to the bearer that the
Queen could not have possibly sent her such a message;
it was neither fitting that she should, 'nor can it be so
sudden, her Majesty being so far from this place. You
should have said the Lady Anne Boleyn . . . and for the
reverence that I made, it was to the altar, to her Maker
and mine . . . they are deceived, and deceive her, who tell
her otherwise.'

It was more than a rebuff, it was a reminder: an intimation in terms of polished condescension to the grand-
daughter of tradesmen that a daughter of kings did not
receive friendly overtures from one who held her at an
unfriendly disadvantage. One can understand why Mary's
resistance drove Anne beyond the bounds of sanely-
calculated fear to exclaim wildly after one of her failures
to have the girl's life, 'she is my death and I am hers;
so I will take care that she shall not laugh at me after
my death.'

All her care proved unavailing to deprive Mary of
that opportunity for laughter had she cared to avail herself
of it. Instead she went on her knees to pray with the best
will she could muster for the repose of the other's soul.
It was Henry who laughed. One wonders which of the
two events would have pained Anne more; there is no
need to ask which would have surprised her more. As

for Mary, even the fact that she confronted far more
pressing danger after her enemy's disappearance than
before did not cure her of the illusion that only her father's
tenderness had stood between her and Anne's murderous
designs. In a sense that was true, but in a strictly limited
sense. The only room for tenderness in Henry's mind by
now was such room as policy allowed. Policy dominated:
the constant search for means and their application to the
end of expanding his area of power and keeping himself
secure within it. It was a pursuit demanding not only a
fertile originality in expedients, but a knowledge of how
to estimate risks, when to wait even to the appearance of
cowardice and when to strike with ruthless and devas-
tating suddenness. It required also a keen insight into
the weaknesses of others that they might be exploited and
into their strength that it might be usefully employed
or made into a cause for their destruction. Sentiment
could be as fatal as illusion; a cold heart was as necessary
as a cool head. In all these respects Henry, beginning as
an amateur in the politicians' art, had discovered a
congenial natural aptitude which, since embarking on his
course of revolutionary change, had developed into a
recognised mastery.

This, far more than his affection, so far constituted
Mary's safeguard. He would never have killed her out
of mere caprice; the mood which Anne so anxiously
sought would never last long enough, nor sufficiently
escape his control, to lead to anything irretrievable. It
was important that Mary should, by taking the Oath of
Succession, publicly admit that the law was right in
setting her aside as a bastard, since she would then
confuse and render harmless the great and—as the story
of her sufferings spread—growing number of her
partisans; but it was even more important for Henry
as yet to keep her as a hostage for his own safety. Rome
had finally pronounced in favour of Catherine, and the

HENRY VIII

This portrait was recovered by infra-red rays from the
portrait originally painted for the Royal College of
Surgeons at its Institution. *Artist unknown*

THOMAS CROMWELL
by Holbein

Pope, after threatening him with excommunication unless he put away Anne, had in fact excommunicated him. What the consequences might be Henry could not foretell. The Pope's spiritual weapons had lost something of their force, the Emperor was occupied with the Turks in the Mediterranean and as always on uneasy terms with France. On the other hand the papacy and France had recently been drawn together by a marriage between the Pope's niece Catherine dei Medici and Francis I's second son, and a movement was clearly afoot to organise a punitive war on Henry and the invasion of England. Behind the movement, clamorously pressing it forward, was the great mass of Christian opinion. High legal authority, by no means all of it papist, was beginning to hold that Henry's conduct, and the edicts condemning it, had cut England off from the comity of Christendom and suspended its rights under the ancient laws of nations and peoples; the Venetian Republic, a historic friend and commercial ally, was reported to be looking for other sources of supply for its wool and other outlets for its cargoes. The situation appeared grave enough to cause Henry, when informed that Mary lay ill at Greenwich, to go there and shout in the hearing of everybody that she was his worst enemy, that on account of her he was on bad terms with most of the Princes of Europe, and to make sure that his words reached her ears. It was curiously reminiscent of his predecessor Henry II's outburst which had led to the murder of St. Thomas à Becket.

But worse was to follow. In July, 1535 the Emperor annihilated the Turkish power in a great battle at Goletta in Tunis. Upon Henry and Cromwell the news, according to a witness, had the effect of causing them to look 'like two dogs that had fallen out of a window', but to most of the world, just then throbbing with rage and horror at the execution of Fisher and More, it brought a

great upsurge of hope. The Pope after a short delay
drew up a Bull of Deprivation for the victorious Emperor
to execute with the active or passive support of France.
At that moment Henry would not only have been relieved to hear of Mary's death but was actually tempted to
bring it about. To the Privy Council he declared, according to Chapuys, that he was tired of living in this state
of constant provocation and alarm and meant to be rid of
both his daughter and his ailing wife as soon as Parliament assembled. When the feelings of his auditors
revealed themselves in contorted faces and even tears he
curtly added that he would not be diverted from his
purpose by such demonstrations if he lost his crown for
it.

Perhaps on this occasion he deceived himself as well
as the agitated councillors; usually his bad tempers were
calculated chiefly to impress others with the lengths to
which he was prepared to go if goaded too far. But though
he would not have hesitated to kill Mary or any one else
to preserve his crown, he would certainly not have risked
it for the satisfaction of showing what he could do when
angry, and by the time he cooled off he knew very well
that for the present it was safer with Mary alive than
dead. To draw up a Bull of Deprivation proved easier
than to persuade Henry's fellow-monarchs to give it
effect. The Emperor was no giddy knight-errant to
fly to the rescue of a wronged female relative on the wings
of a papal blessing. There was not only France to be
seduced from attacking him while his forces were
engaged elsewhere—this he was trying to accomplish
with the prospect of Mary's hand and a share in her
future throne for Francis's third son—there was also
the agreement of his Netherlands subjects to be secured
for an enterprise which might jeopardise their valuable
English trade, and most important of all, there were
schemes to be set going for the fusion of all the dis-

contented in England to prepare a welcome for the Spanish armies when they arrived. Till all this had been put in train Henry's supreme emergency would not have arisen; only when it had would Mary's.

There were already stirrings, particularly in the North, where the old religion was still strong; there would be even more when the government announced the further changes and repressions already in contemplation. The year 1535, owing to bad weather—it was noted that it had rained steadily since the execution of the Carthusians—promised to yield less than half the annual harvest of grain. England might soon be dependent for her food on imports from France and the Low Countries, ruled by potential enemies whose ambassadors were already urging them to refuse it. Meantime the Crown's income was gravely impaired owing to the inability of its tenants to pay rents, and Henry being driven to further impositions on his people as well as towards the spoliation of the monasteries which was to transform disaffection into active rebellion. The shape of things to come was already visible: the northern magnates were in secret touch—though not entirely secret to Henry's agents—with the Imperial representatives for help in the form of arms and eventually armies. If and when the internal rising occurred and the Spanish hosts mustered on the opposite shores of the North Sea would come the time to threaten to kill Mary the moment a foreign soldier set foot on English soil, and if the threat failed to stave his enemies off, to make it good so as to divide and disorganise them by rendering hopeless from the start the paramount object which joined them together. Until then she could be used to counter their preliminary diplomatic manoeuvres and Francis I was set to musing on how well he might do with how little risk both for Mary and his eldest son the Dauphin by fulfilling their old contract of marriage.

Political motives rather than private feelings defined also Henry's attitude towards her sufferings. He would not see her himself, despite her repeated pleas, because that would signify to the world that he had given his countenance to her rejection of his laws. Nor would he let her see Catherine, in the face of the most piteous appeals from both, and especially from Catherine, whose tear-splashed pages are almost too heart-breaking to read. Gravely ill herself, with good reason to suspect that she had not much longer to live, she gathered from the little notes smuggled to her or the occasional visitors who managed to penetrate to Kimbolton that Mary was also suffering from a complication of illnesses aggravated by nervous depression and neglect. In vain Catherine besought Cromwell 'to tell his Majesty it was my wish that he should send her where I am, as the comfort and cheerfulness she would have with me would be half the cure.' If Henry entertained, as she had heard, 'some suspicion of her security'—the fear lest Mary escape or be kidnapped—'I offer my person as security that if such a thing be attempted, he may do justice upon me as the most traitorous woman that ever was born'. If all else failed, she would be grateful to have Mary at least near her so as to receive more frequent and trustworthy news and pledge her word not to attempt to visit her—a feat for which, as she remarked, she had neither the physical strength nor the material means 'even if she were but a mile from me'.

From Cromwell she turned to Chapuys, a less dubious advocate, and begged him to ask for an audience of Henry so as to 'say to his Highness that there is no need for any other person but myself to nurse her; that I will put her in my own bed where I sleep and watch her when needful'. Chapuys went and was courteously refused. To bring together the two women for whom Henry's subjects were already too eager to show their love separately would be to set up a sort of joint shrine of disaffection for multitudes to flock to on every conceivable pretext. Moreover, he told Chapuys frankly, though he was prepared to do everything possible for Mary's health, he could not run the risk of her being carried off by the Emperor's agents according to a scheme he had heard was afoot. He blamed Catherine for undermining her natural obedience, and poured scorn on the suggestion that she be placed again in charge of the old Countess of Salisbury, 'a fool of no experience', in whose care she might die whereas her present governess was sensible and knowledgeable. That he was at least sincere in his concern for Mary's health he attested by not only sending his own physician but allowing Catherine's, who knew her well, to attend her, with the proviso that he see her only in the presence of witnesses and speak nothing but English to her. In addition he sent her two presents of money.

Had Henry been privileged to read Chapuys' correspondence he could not have handled the colloquy more shrewdly. The ambassador could scarcely counter Henry's objections to a change of governesses since he was too well aware, and had informed his superiors of the real, unspoken reason against it: Mary might easily be poisoned while in charge of her friends by one of Anne's minions without it being possible to fix the guilt on any one, whereas Lady Shelton had been terrified out of her wits, not least by Chapuys himself, at the dire penalties that would be exacted of her should such a thing happen under her responsibility. Even less could Chapuys allay Henry's fears of Mary's escape, since that was precisely what he was doing his best to contrive. He felt certain that an internal upheaval was coming to be followed by Imperial intervention which he was in fact urging, and recognised that Mary would be in extreme peril in Henry's hands but an invaluable asset in the Emperor's.

It was not an easy matter to arrange. Besides being closely watched, Mary was not sure of her own mind. At times she would beg, through one of the servants he managed to put into communication with her, that 'for the love of God' he would 'remove her from the danger which is otherwise inevitable', at others she resolved with equal desperation that she would not abandon her mother nor seem to abandon the cause for which they stood. Now Chapuys would press her, now 'because I see the thing is difficult, I keep her in hope of a remedy by some other means, and endeavour to remove her suspicion that foul play is intended against her'. Yet his heart and soul were in the business: 'You may well consider,' he wrote the Emperor, 'what solace and pastime she can have with those about her hearing them desire her death, by which, they say the world would be at peace and they discharged of the pain and trouble they have taken about her.' The practical difficulties were aggravated by the fact that the attempt could not take place at night since it was most important 'that it should appear as little as possible that it was by her consent, for the sake of her own honour and the less to irritate the King her father.' At length Chapuys worked out a plan for her to be surprised while moving from one house to another, carried to a rowboat on the Thames and thence to a Spanish galleon waiting off Gravesend. But before the plan could be put into execution Mary was suddenly removed forty miles away to Hunsdon in Hertfordshire and there fell seriously ill again.

She had recovered sufficiently to take renewed interest in the plans for her escape when, at the beginning of January, 1536, she heard the news of her mother's death. Though it had long been expected, it was received with general horror and surprise. It was too opportune, so far

as nature went too premature—for Catherine was only 50
—and Mary was far from alone in believing that it was
in fact unnatural. The unskilled postmortem did little
to allay the popular suspicion, although the symptoms,
according to modern pathologists, would have justified
a diagnosis of cancer of the heart. Mary, prostrated by
her loss, felt certain, as did many others, that she was
marked to follow, but cared little; for the first time she
prayed to be allowed to die.

It was not a prayer of which Catherine would have
approved either on worldly or spiritual grounds. In the
letter written to Henry from her deathbed there is no
suggestion of his having hastened her death, nor of any
cause whatever to despair that right would ultimately
be done to Mary:

'My most Dear Lord, King and Husband,
    The hour of my death now approaching, I cannot
choose but, out of the love I bear you, advise you of
your soul's health, which you ought to prefer before
all considerations of the world of flesh whatsoever.
For which yet you have cast me into many calamities,
and yourself into many troubles. But I forgive you all;
and pray God to do so likewise. For the rest I commend
unto you Mary our daughter, beseeching you to be a
good father to her, as I have heretofore desired. I must
intreat you also, to respect my Maids, and give them
in marriage, which is not much, seeing they be but
three, and to all my other servants a year's pay besides
their due, lest otherwise they should be unprovided
for. Lastly I make this vow, that mine eyes desire you
above all things. Farewell.'

Her prayers were not altogether in vain. Not only did
Henry bury her with reverence at Peterborough, devoting her small estate 'towards her funeral chiefly' and
the balance upon 'those who deserved recompense' from

her, but in his will, drawn up not long before his death, made his final dispositions in favour of the daughter 'lawfully begotten upon the body of our entirely beloved wife Queen Katharine.'

But that was ten years later. Henry's immediate feeling was one of relief that he had been delivered from the danger of war; now that he was a widower, so far as Catherine was concerned, no one could seriously question the legality of his marriage to Anne, to the extent, certainly, of making a *casus belli* out of it, and if Anne, who had been pregnant since the previous autumn, should be delivered of a son, the succession would have been settled beyond possibility of question. Official attention shifted so completely from Mary for a time that Chapuys thought she might no longer be molested; at worst she might be required to recognise Anne as Queen, and in that event he advised her simply to play the part of the newly bereaved orphan anxious only to be left alone with her grief and her prayers—not a difficult rôle for her to maintain—and if her conscience forbade her to recognise Anne, to disclaim all knowledge of the law except to insist that it had never been the practice in England to take an oath of allegiance to queens. The policy was not one to commend itself to Anne who, as if tormented by a premonition that she must regulate matters with Mary before her confinement, continued in a kind of breathless frenzy to cajole and threaten her with what she would do when the birth of her son had made her own position invincible.

On 29th January, the day of Catherine's funeral, she miscarried of a male infant. For her it was the end and she knew it. She tried to put the blame on her uncle the Duke of Norfolk for having too abruptly broken the news to her of Henry's fall from a horse. Henry simply jeered and passed to Cromwell the task of finding the quickest and most effective way of getting rid of her. The long

and ignominious list of accusations was put together—
adulteries with lovers of all grades and degrees of kinship
—her derision of Henry's clothing and manners—her
persecution of his late wife and elder daughter . . . Cromwell overlooked nothing. Even execration was stilled for a
moment by a kind of incredulous horror. Meanwhile
Chapuys pondered anxiously the portents for Mary and
was not reassured. He took at their proper value Henry's
determination to have an heir and in the last resort to
have his own way. He knew, as the country in general
as yet did not, of Henry's interest in Jane Seymour, the
young woman whom he had met the previous autumn
at her father's house in Wiltshire. With another wife in
prospect and two useless female orphans on his hands,
it might well be that Henry would decide to tidy what
was becoming a very complicated situation before making
a fresh start towards an uncertain future. Once more
Chapuys tried to get Mary out of the country whence she
could assert her claims with safety under her cousin the
Emperor's protection, again he was hampered not only
by the practical difficulties but by her own divided mind,
which at one moment made her so eager to do what he
proposed that she declared her readiness to cross the
Channel in a sieve if need be, at another so indifferent
to her own safety as to resolve to remain where she was if
thereby she might bring comfort to the vast number of
those looking to her to restore the old faith in England
and help at the same time in restoring the 'soul's health'
of her father.

She was still undecided when she heard of Anne's
execution on 19th May and of her father's remarriage,
amidst most unsuitable rejoicings, a few days later.

CHAPTER FOUR

Henry's Success

A week after Anne's execution Mary wrote to Cromwell:

'Master Secretary,

I would have been a suitor to you before this time, to have been a mean for me to the King's Grace my father, to have obtained his Grace's blessing and favour; but I perceived that nobody durst speak for me, as long as that woman lived which is now gone, whom I pray our Lord of his great mercy to forgive. Wherefor, now she is gone, I am the bolder to write to you, as she which taketh you for one of my chief friends. And therefore I desire you, for the love of God, to be a suitor for me to the King's Grace, to have his blessing and license to write unto his Grace, which shall be a great comfort to me, as God knoweth, who have you ever more in his holy keeping. Moreover, I must desire you to accept mine evil writing. For I have not done so much this two year or more, nor could not have found the means to do it at this time, but my Lady Kingston's being here. At Hounsdon, the 26th of May.

By your loving friend
Marye.'

Perhaps it was the hope of some such consummation that accounted for her waning interest in Chapuys' preparations to spirit her abroad. With her rooted conviction that Anne had been the source of her troubles, his notion that Anne's death boded ill rather than good for her must have seemed paradoxical. So it would certainly have seemed to a world confidently awaiting a turn in her fortunes that went well beyond the grant of her modest requests. Even in the innermost circles of the court it was anticipated that Henry, his matrimonial affairs at last happily in order, would moderate the excesses of a policy so full of danger for himself and everybody else, in due course make his peace with Rome and in the meantime restore Mary to her obvious place as his heiress presumptive until such time as Queen Jane should supersede her with an heir-apparent. As early as March, half way between Catherine's death and Anne's, Cromwell was seen to touch his cap when referring to her. A little later his fellow-Secretary Pate gave expression to the hope that the King 'would not suffer that redolent flower to be deprived of the sun's warmth and wither away'. Some gentleman of the Privy Chamber risked, and incurred, Henry's displeasure by openly predicting that she would soon be restored after consenting to some agreed form of regret for her contumacy, and various ladies of the court hurried to make application to enter her service. It was known that powerful intercession was being made on her behalf not only by the Emperor personally but by Henry's new bride in terms so warm as to draw upon herself his reproach for giving less than due consideration to her own expected offspring.

His response to Mary's overture was prompt, and if it fell short of her sympathisers' expectations, it more than realised her own. He authorised Cromwell, (whose letter is lost, but its gist is clear from her answer to it), to inform her that she might write him as she desired; more than that, to hold out hopes, which she fervently acknowledged in the answer referred to, written on 30th May, 'that by your wisdom, help and means his Grace shall not only withdraw his displeasure . . . but also license me to come into his presence.' Her delight, her gratitude to

Cromwell for his good offices, were inexpressible. She apologised for 'this short and evil-written letter' due to 'the rheum in my head which will suffer me to write no more at this time'—in fact she was also suffering, according to her physician, from gastric influenza—and swore that if Cromwell would continue to act as her 'most humble petitioner', she would do as much for him 'in like case (I take God to be my judge) . . . if the same did ever lie in my power.' Unfortunately for him it did not when his turn came. Then she set herself to the composition of the letter to her father, which she finished two days later. The thought and trouble and yearning that went into it perhaps account, no less than her illness, for the time it took; the deference which the age demanded of child to parent and subject to sovereign sufficiently account for the language:

'In as humble and lowly a manner as is possible for a child to use to her father & sovereign lord, I beseech your Grace of your daily blessing, which is my chief desire in this world. And in the same humble wise (ac)knowledging all the offences that I have done unto your Grace, since I had first discretion to offend unto this hour, I pray your Grace, in the honour of God, & for your fatherly pity to forgive them; for the which I am as sorry as any creature living; & next unto God, I do & will submit me in all things to your goodness and pleasure, to do with me whatsoever shall please your Grace, humbly beseeching your Highness to consider that I am a woman & your child, who hath committed her soul to God, & her body to be ordered in this world as it shall stand with your pleasure; whose order & direction whatsoever it shall please yr Highness to limit & direct to me I shall most humbly & willingly stand content to follow, obey & accomplish in all points. And so

in the lowliest manner that I can, I beseech your
Grace to accept me, your humble daughter, which
doth not only rejoice to hear the comfortable tidings,
not only to me, but to all your Grace's realm, concerning the marriage which is between your Grace
& the Queen, now being your Grace's wife, my
mother-in-law. The hearing whereof caused nature
to constrain me to be an humble suitor to your Grace,
to be so good & gracious lord and father to me,
as to give me leave to wait upon the Q., & to do
her grace such service as shall please her to command
me, which my heart shall be as ready & obedient to
fulfil (next unto your Grace) as the most humble
servant that she hath. Trusting in your Grace's mercy
to come into your Presence, which ever hath & shall
be the greatest comfort that I can have within this
world; having also a full hope in your Grace's natural
pity, which you have allwayes used as much or more
than any Prince christened, that your Grace will
show the same upon me your most humble & obedient
daughter; who daily prayeth God to have your Grace
in his holy keeping, with a long life, & as much
honour as ever had King & to send your Grace
shortly a Prince, whereof no living creature shall
more rejoice or heartlier pray for continually than I,
as my duty bindeth me. From Houndson, the first
day of June

By your Grace's most humble
daughter & handmaid
Marye'

A week passed without bringing any answer. Racked
with suspense and almost sleepless with pain, unable to
fathom the meaning of the silence and the curious looks
in the hostile faces surrounding her, she decided that she
could bear it no longer and wrote Cromwell again:

'Good Master Secretary,

I think so long to hear some comfort from the King's Grace my father, whereby I may perceive his Grace of his princely goodness and fatherly pity to have accepted my letter and withdrawn his displeasure towards me, that nature moveth me to be so bold to send his Grace a token, which my servant this bearer hath to deliver to you, or to any other at your appointment, desiring you (for the love of God) to find some means by your wisdom and goodness that the King may be so good and gracious a lord to me as to send me a token . . .'

Then, unable to await his answer in order to learn how her present was received, on the following day she addressed a second letter to Henry:

'In as humble and lowly manner as is possible for me I beseech your Grace of your daily blessing, by the obtaining whereof, with also to write unto your Grace, albeit I understand to mine inestimable comfort that your princely goodness and fatherly pity hath forgiven all mine offence and withdrawn your dreadful displeasure, long time conceived against me, yet shall my joy never be full nor my hope satisfied unto such time as your Grace vouchsafe more sensibly to express your reconciled heart, love and favour towards me, either by your gracious letters or else some token till I may by your merciful calling and sufferance attain the fruition of your most desired presence; for the which I humbly desire your Grace to pardon me, though I trouble you with my continual suit and rude writing.'

She ended with a message for his new wife and a prayer that 'God shortly (to) send a Prince between you both, which shall be gladder tidings to me than I can express in writing.'

Not least amongst the elements in her impending agony was sheer surprise at how little she had understood her father's mind. She had supposed—indeed had been led to suppose—that Henry was only waiting for her to express suitable regret for her disobedience in her mother's and Anne's lifetime before taking her back into his affection. Now she was to learn that she had been encouraged to ask for bread in order that her father might offer her a stone. The first definite hint came to her, as usual, from Chapuys. On 6th June he reported to the Emperor a visit from Cromwell in the course of which the Secretary remarked how much Mary's letters had pleased Henry and his new Queen. It was now proposed, he went on, to ask her to copy word for word and sign an act of submission to be drawn up for her by Cromwell himself 'in the most honourable and reasonable form that could be'. Mary had already been apprised of this by an unnamed lady on Henry's instructions, the Secretary further declared—an assertion not necessarily nor even probably true—and asked the Ambassador to cooperate by sending a man armed with a certified translation of the document into Latin to urge Mary to sign it. Chapuys, suspecting an attempt at 'birdcatching', contrived instead to send a secret intimation to Mary.

Almost simultaneously, on 8th June, a second Act of Succession replaced the first. It pronounced both Mary and Elizabeth to be illegitimate and made it high treason to hold otherwise. It also gave Henry the right to leave the Crown by will to 'any person . . . of his most Royal Blood' in the event of his death without lawful issue—a proviso widely interpreted as a step towards the Duke of Richmond's nomination to succeed should Jane do no better in the matter of a son than had her predecessors. If this was really what Henry had in mind, his sudden insistence on Mary's instant and outright submission to the terms of the Act becomes explicable on the simple

theory that he wished to eliminate her as a possible rival
to her natural half-brother. But providence apparently
disapproved of adultery as much as of marriage with
deceased brothers' wives, for the Duke died the following
month at the age of 17 . . . too soon for Henry to exercise
his discretion under the Act in the boy's favour, too late
to help in determining whether he ever really meant to
do so.

For by the time of Richmond's death the conflict of
wills between Mary and her father was over. Had he
died seven weeks earlier and Henry as a result desisted
from his attempt to force Mary's submission, then the
belief that he was acting in the Duke's interest would
have much to be said for it. But there are good reasons
for thinking that his conduct towards Mary had nothing
to do with Richmond: that he in fact intended all along
to concede her rightful place in the order of succession,
as he ultimately did, but on his own conditions. Few
despots have ever excelled Henry in the ability to assess
public opinion and estimate from it what he could or
could not ultimately do. It is unlikely that this instinct
would not have warned him that no mere legislative
enactment, by its nature earthly and ephemeral, could of
itself make or unmake legitimacy, a thing of quasi-
supernatural origin in the eyes of the English people as
the adventurer who later tried to rob Mary of her birthright by legal act swiftly and disastrously learned. For
Henry the first consideration was necessarily the continu-
ation of his dynasty by peaceful succession. If Jane
bore him a son all would be well: it was scarcely conceivable that Mary would dispute, or find any one to support
her in disputing, that son's title, and therefore improbable
that Henry was prepared to resort to extremes to avert
a contingency so remote. But if Jane failed to produce
an heir and Henry took advantage of a parliamentary
statute to leave his crown to his bastard, he could be

absolutely certain of bequeathing England a civil war.
The only reasonable alternative, then, however unsatisfactory, was Mary—provided he could place it beyond
her and her supporters' power to upset the peace of his
kingdom while he was alive and Jane's son still unborn.

That he was seeking such safeguards during the
unrest provoked by his religious revolution rather than
Mary's final elimination is indicated by various evidences.
Sir Anthony Browne and Sir Francis Brian, arrested at
this time for saying that he intended, failing issue by
Jane, to name Mary his heir once she had submitted,
told their examiners that this was common talk amongst
their colleagues of the Privy Chamber, a body of men
very close to the King's confidence; their arrest suggests
the possibility that they were punished for prematurely
divulging his mind hoping thereby to force his hand.
In answer to one of Chapuys' protests at the violation of
Mary's rights, Cromwell insisted that she was making
her own difficulties: if she would refrain from irritating
Henry by refusing what was required of her, her friends
would have no further reason to complain of his provision
for her. And though Chapuys remained sceptical, it
is a fact that Cromwell openly gave it as his opinion that,
even if the marriage of Henry and Catherine was originally
invalid, Mary might still be regarded as legitimate
because it had been contracted in good faith. Henry
himself told the Emperor, in answer to the latter's
intercession, that 'as to the legitimation of our daughter
Mary, if she will submit to our grace, not wrestling
against the determination of our laws, we will acknowledge
and use her as our daughter'—not, however, as Henry
was careful to add, because but despite the uninvited
meddling of relatives-in-law in his affairs, since 'God
has . . . given us wisdom, policy and other graces in most
plentiful sort to direct' them by. When finally it came to
the actual form of submission demanded of Mary, it

will be seen that it did not in fact disqualify her under the terms of the Act of Succession but left Henry free, if he so desired, to fulfil the promise implied in his statement to the Emperor.

Mary's second letter he ignored like the first, but from Cromwell there arrived a prompt acknowledgment of hers to him of 7th June enclosing the draft of a letter which she was to copy, sign and return to him. It repeated, in language of even more abject humility, her 'hearty repentance' and desire for some 'gracious letter, token or message, as an earnest of his forgiveness' and ultimately 'the fruition of your most noble presence', and ended with the promise 'henceforward and wholly, next to God Almighty, to put my state, contrivance and living in your gracious mercy, and likewise to accept the condition of your disposition and appointment, whatsoever it shall be.' This copy she sealed and returned to Cromwell along with his original draft enclosed in a letter pointing out 'that I have followed my advice and counsel, and will do in all things concerning my duty to the King's Grace (God and my conscience not offended), for I take you for one of my chief friends, next unto his Grace and the Queen . . .'

And then suddenly something flares up, as if the paper had by some miracle become incandescent. Some would in fact allow the miracle and speak of the intrusion of grace. For submissiveness blazes into defiance; the tiny figure scratching away at her monotonous, stilted phrases in her pathetic attempt to strike the precise combination which will gain the approval of her elders, becomes at this point as if possessed, transformed, and quietly lays down her challenge to Cromwell, to Henry and to all the massed forces of the world at their command. So far and no further. Of her own will, as well as at Cromwell's direction, she had striven, and would continue to strive, to express the love she felt and the duty she owed towards her father and her king according to her own inclination and the teaching she had received. But it was God who had awarded him the right to receive them, and it was her own conscience, the gift of God, which must decide in the event of a conflict between Him and any mere creature, including the King her father, which had the first claim upon them. 'Wherefore I desire you,' her letter to Cromwell went on,

'for the passion which Christ suffered for you and me, and as my very trust is in you, that you will find means through your great wisdom that I will not be moved to agree to any further entry in this matter than I have done. For I assure you, by the faith I owe to God, I have done the uttermost that my conscience will suffer me; and I do neither desire nor intend to do less than I have done. But if I be put to any more (I am plain with you as my great friend) my said conscience will in no ways suffer me to consent thereunto. And this point except, you nor any other shall be so much desirous to have me obey the King as I shall be ready to fulfil the same. . . . Sir, I beseech you for the love of God to take in good worth this rude letter. For I would not have troubled you so much at this time, but that the end of your letter caused me a little to fear that I shall have more business hereafter . . .
From Hounsdon the X of June, etc.

If to wish her well according to his lights constituted friendship, then Thomas Cromwell was, as Mary took him to be, one of her chief friends within the narrow circle of power. Unlike several of his colleagues he had no desire to see her killed: not that he shrank from killing in its proper place, but because his realistic, orderly intelligence grasped the inadvisability of creating a void in the succession with all the complications that must ensue. But Mary's scruples could not but fill him

with fear and impatience. Henry had entrusted him with
the task of securing her submission, and he well remembered what had happened to his late master Wolsey
for failing in the very similar task of securing Catherine's
submission and through her the Pope's. Henry had no
need to roar at him (as Henry probably did, with a cuff
on the ear for emphasis) that he did not like Mary's
interpolation into his draft of the phrase 'wholly next
to God Almighty'; it was the sort of exception Cromwell
more than any other man had taught him not to like.
The interesting wastage of the qualifying phrase 'so
far as the law of God allows' between the first submission
of the clergy and the formal Act of Supremacy was a
choice example of the Secretary's success in this respect.
In themselves Cromwell neither liked nor disliked such
tags; he merely regarded them as meaningless, though
potentially dangerous with so many fanatics about. 'The
passion which Christ suffered for you and me' had
happened too long ago to concern him very much in
dealing with the here and now. This is not to say that
he doubted the basic tenets of Christianity; had there
been any ground for supposing that he did he would
not have held office nor, very probably, held on very
long to life. But it is hard to imagine a far-off God in
heaven enlisting the whole of his mind, energy, devotion
or even worship; for the full deployment of these he had
need of a more immediate deity whom he could see and
touch. Not being a simple credulous idolater but a modern
man free of ancient superstitions and illusions, it was
perhaps only natural that, for the sake of an effective
understanding of him, he would prefer one he had made
himself. In a sense he had made Henry, in whom he saw
the embodiment of the particular attribute inseparable
from his notion of divinity—the ability to wield power
unalloyed by scruple or self-doubt.

In his youth he had travelled in Italy in search of

profit and experience, under both of which heads he would
have included his perusal in manuscript of the work
which had since in its printed form become the political
gospel of the wide-awake man of affairs, Machiavelli's
The Prince. Back in England he married well and, after
supporting the early uncertainties of a solicitor's practice
upon a solid income from the wool-trade, thrived so
remarkably that in time a large proportion of the great
and powerful were his clients bound to him by the secrets
they had communicated and the money he had lent them.
Election to Parliament followed as a matter of course,
then an invitation by Wolsey, who had an eye for a
rising man, to enter his service, whence, after the latter's
downfall, he passed smoothly into Henry's, and so by
swift stages to wielding most of the Cardinal's power as
well as filling many of his offices together with several
new ones, including the vicegerency of Henry's Church.
Unlike Wolsey, he had no allegiance but to Henry.
Against the absolute and unrestricted authority of the
wearer of the English Crown, any claims put forward on
behalf of the unity of Christendom, the primacy of the
Pope, the moral law itself, he was prepared to reject as
irrelevant, in a manner of speaking heretical. Deeming
money to be the main bulwark of power, he had pledged
himself to make Henry the richest prince in Europe
and was endeavouring to carry out the pledge no matter
how or at whose expense; in order to secure Henry
against all possible opposition or even criticism, he had
without compunction spun the legal web which had
fatally entangled not only the humble and unsuspecting
but the wary and resourceful. So consistently had he
preached and so ably practised his doctrine that the King
could do no wrong—unless to himself through weakness
or shortsightedness—that Henry had without a quibble
adopted it as his own. Deity and worshipper were well
satisfied with each other. If Henry occasionally chastised

his servant, he also lavishly rewarded him; if Cromwell
was frightened of his master's displeasure—the only
thing in heaven or earth he was frightened of—he
rejoiced, like a true religious believer, in the glory with
which he was able to vest him. Other less favoured wor-
shippers hated Cromwell as a too-successful monopolist,
but most of those who had to do business with him found
it hard to resist the unquenchable good humour, the
readiness to listen sympathetically, that radiated from
the large coarse face with its undistinguished features and
quivering cascade of chins.

His reception of Mary's prayerful little ultimatum was
masterly. He neither threatened nor argued, knowing well
from past experience and observation that upon a character like hers, so rooted in a simple set of convictions and
so determined to do right, the only effect of threats
would be to stiffen resolution and of arguments to beget
eager counter-arguments. But she was very young,
terribly alone and piteously eager for the approval
of the one being on earth of whose rightness she felt as
sure as her own, her father. For so adroit a practical
psychologist as Cromwell it was not too difficult to detect
an obvious conflict and cultivate in her mind a subtle
confusion. How could she dream, he asked in his reply
to her letter of 10th June (this letter too is lost, but its
tone as well as its contents are again easy to infer from
her answer of the 13th), that her father of all men would
expect her to say or do anything wrong? And by what
pretension did she venture to set her own immature
judgment against his as to what God required of her?
With friendly severity he advised her to mend her language lest Henry be forced to suppose that she was
opposing him out of sheer unfilial perversity.

He carried his point. She was too tired, ill and perplexed to dispute it further since it appeared to involve
no issue of principle: for how could she believe, still less

urge, that Henry's insight into the divine will was inferior to, or that his motives were less elevated than, her
own? 'Good Master Secretary', she wrote,

> 'I do thank you with all my heart for the pain and suit
> you have had for me, for the which I think myself
> very much bound to you. And whereas I do perceive
> by your letters that you do mislike mine exception
> in my letter to the King's Grace, I assure you I did not
> mean it as you take it. For I do not mistrust that the
> King's goodness will move me to do anything which
> should offend God and my conscience; but that which
> I did write was only by the reason of continual custom,
> for I have always used, both in writing and speaking,
> to except God in all things.
>
> Nevertheless, because you have exhorted me to
> write to his Grace again, and I cannot devise what I
> should write more but your own last copy, without
> adding or minishing, therefore I do send you by this
> bearer my servant the same word for word; and it is
> unsealed because I cannot bear to write another copy.
> For the pain in my head and teeth hath troubled
> me so sore these two or three days, and doth yet so
> continue, that I have very small rest day or night
> . . .'

Enclosed with this she returned her copy of his draft,
as she said, repeating all the fulsome, to later ears nause-
ating, professions of repentance and obedience, with the
offending phrase omitted and God invoked only as her
judge that she meant 'to use myself so from henceforth
as your Grace shall have cause to think your mercy and
pity well extended unto me . . .'

She may well have thought that this was the end, that
the way was now open to her father's embrace. It was,
in fact, but the end of a stage, the stage described in
certain modern police circles which the Secretary would

undeniably have graced as 'the softening-up process'.
By means of it Mary had been brought to utter language
of submission the better to subdue her for performing the
actual act. Instead of an answer from Cromwell, or better
yet Henry, to her letter of 13th June, she received
almost immediately a delegation headed by the Duke of
Norfolk and comprising amongst others the Earl of
Sussex and the Bishop of Chester. The instructions which
they carried set forth so well Henry's own view of Mary,
of himself and of the differences between them that they
are worth printing in full.

'First, whereas the said Lady Mary hath sundry ways,
with long continuance, shown herself so obstinant
towards the King's Majesty, her Sovereign Lord &
Father, and so disobedient to his laws, conceived and
made upon the most just, virtuous and godly grounds,
that as the wilful disobedience thereof seemeth a
monster in Nature, so unless the mercy of his Highness
had been most abundantly extended to her, by the
course of his Grace's laws and the force of his justice
she endangered herself so far that it was greatly to
his Highness's regret and hearty sorrow to see and
perceive how little she esteemeth the same; extending
to the loss of his favour, the loss of her honour, the
loss of her life, and undoubtedly to the indignation
of Almighty God: for that she neither obeyeth her
father and sovereign nor his just and virtuous laws
aforesaid. And that of late, nevertheless, calling to
remembrance her transgressions and offences in this
part towards God, her father and Sovereign lord the
King's Highness, she hath written to the same three
sundry letters, containing a declaration of her repentance conceived for the premises, with such an humble
and simple submission, as she appeareth not only to
submit wholly and without exception (especially

by the last letter) to the laws, but also for her state and condition to put herself only to his Grace's mercy; nothing desiring but mercy and forgiveness for her offences, with a reconciliation to his Grace's favour.

Albeit his Majesty has been so greatly handled and used by her . . . that the like would enforce any private person to abandon forever such an unkind and in-obedient child from their grace and favour; yet such is his Majesty's gracious and divine nature, such is his clemency and pity, such his merciful inclination and princely heart, that as he hath been ever ready to take pity and compassion of all offenders, repentantly calling and crying for the same; so in case he may perceive the same to be in the said Lady Mary's heart, which she hath put in pen and writing, his Highness considering the imbecility of her sex, being the same is frail, inconstant and easy to be persuaded by simple counsel, can be right well contented to remit unto her part of his displeasure. And therefore hath at this time, for the certain knowledge of her heart and stomach, sent unto her his said cousin with others to demand and enquire of her certain questions. . . .'

to which they—that is Norfolk and his colleagues—were to bring back Mary's answers.

1. Will she recognise Henry as King and obey his Laws?

2. 'Also set forth, advance and maintain the same?'

3. Recognise him as Supreme Head of the Church of England and repudiate the Pope and his Laws?

4. Acknowledge his marriage with her mother by God's Law and man's law to be unlawful?

5. Declare 'for what cause, and by whose motion and means, she hath continued and remained in her obstinacy so long; and who did enbolden or animate

her thereunto, with other circumstances thereof pertaining.'

6. 'Also what is the cause that at this present time, rather than at any other heretofore, she doth submit herself.'

The third and fourth were, of course, the essential ones to which the first and second were merely introductory. If Mary accepted the general principle that Henry had the right to institute laws which it was her duty not only to obey but actively to maintain, it became the more difficult for her to repudiate the particular laws embodied in the Acts of Supremacy and Succession. It is hard to see, however, why she should have been required to affirm that she recognised him as King, a fact that never had nor ever could have occurred to her to question, unless it was feared that a rebellion might be raised in her name to call it into question, when her own acknowledgment would be useful and perhaps decisive. All the more was it imperative that she should recognise him as Supreme Head, for if the rebellion did occur, it would certainly have as its principal motive the desire to undo his religious settlement with which the majority of his subjects were out of sympathy. But there may have been, and probably was, another and even stronger reason for the Crown's insistence on this point. If she forfeited her rights to the succession by her answer to the fourth question, the trouble taken to gain her consent to the religious settle-ment seems almost superfluous. As a private, self-discredited person, her refusal could not have been much of an embarrassment unless the King's enemies chose to exploit it by repudiating her avowal of illegitimacy and raising a rebellion as feared, when she could have been expeditiously done to death by the ordinary process of law. But if Henry and his advisers had it in mind that she might one day succeed him, then it became of the utmost consequence that she should be bound in every possible way to confirm the work of his reign.

The last two questions were an obvious afterthought apparently designed to test how far Mary was now prepared to co-operate. That they were not very seriously intended would seem to be evident from the fact that they were not pressed to a conclusion after Mary had declined to answer them out of concern for those who had helped and encouraged her: doubtless the Crown knew the answers already. In the event the chief interest in those questions lies less in what they asked than in what they presumed. Henry and Cromwell clearly believed that the softening-up process was complete; that she was now prepared to respond to their specific demands with her instant and total submisison.

How mistaken they were their envoys quickly discovered. She made no difficulty about answering the first and second questions in the affirmative but flatly declined to do so with regard to the third and fourth; the satisfaction she had been willing to give in the matter of her humility to Henry she evidently regarded as in no way inconsistent with her previous warning to Cromwell. Her visitors, falling into the error which the Secretary had astutely avoided, condescended to argue. She had her replies ready and made them with spirit. They were the familiar ones, radiations of the teaching which had been wound into the core of her being. To deny or even to question the King's authority over her as his daughter and subject would, she readily acknowledged, be nothing less than blasphemous, since it admittedly and by express Scriptural warrant came, as her interlocutors urged, from God. But the very admission set the limits to that authority, since they too had been set by God, Who had placed the responsibilities of free will upon the individual conscience under the guidance of the Holy Ghost and delegated certain special authority, visibly and audibly through His Son, to the successor of Saint Peter, within whose spiritual domain fell the sacrament of marriage.

The whole thing hung together: to deny one part was to deny the other. Her interlocutors knew this as well as she, for they had been brought up, if not all of them as thoroughly as she, to a respect for the same system of distinctions and coherences. Unable to confute her, they became annoyed with her, 'told her that since she was so unnatural as to oppose the King so obstinately, they could scarcely believe that she was his bastard, and if she was their daughter they would beat her and knock her head so violently against the wall that they would make it soft as baked apples.' It is interesting to note that they stressed her short-comings as a daughter rather than as a subject, since as subjects themselves they perhaps hesitated to emphasise the duty of unconditional sub-mission to the power of the State which it would be the task of the future to make intellectually palatable. After a few parting epithets, including that of 'traitress', coupled with the threat that she should be punished as such, Norfolk and his fellows returned to lay their report before the Privy Council.

For a week that body, purged of two of its members accounted her sympathisers, gave its undivided attention to the problem of what to do with her. Some urged that she should be brought summarily to trial, others that she be given one last chance to change her mind. When after several days' debate the former view seemed about to prevail the judges were called in, according to custom, for technical advice, but turned the scales by declining, in spite of black looks and threatening words from the majority, to lend their assistance until Mary had been notified in writing of the precise demands to which she was expected to submit and had formally refused to do so. Meantime an order had been given to 'her gouvernante ... not to allow any one to speak to her, and that she and another should never lose sight of her day and night'. The two or three devoted women who had been left to serve her were removed and after a short period of captivity compelled to take the two statutory oaths forswearing her.

Utterly alone except for the cold and silent observation of her custodians, Mary entered into the crisis of her agony. It had been possible to keep up hope while she had faith to sustain her, but now she began to feel even that slipping from her. To refute the shallow insincerities of her recent inquisitors with the august platitudes transmitted to her by a thousand years of thought and experience had been easy enough. But to be self-convincing is not necessarily to be right; it may on the contrary amount to no more than being self-righteous; conscience so often speaks with such different utterance in the heat of debate and in the still watches. Mary, left to grapple in solitude with a moral problem demanding the fortitude of a hero and the insight of a saint for its correct solution—one little different in substance and no way inferior in magnitude and perplexity to those presented to Antigone and Joan of Arc—felt herself beginning to waver and doubt.

What if, after all, she were wrong? If it was mere presumption on her part to suppose that she, an inexperienced girl of 20, could pit her understanding of the will of God against the combined judgment of the King and his ministers as well as some of the ablest and most learned of the bishops and other distinguished professors of religion? She could hardly have helped remembering as her self-examination proceeded her mother's caution, at once so loving and so stern, against the impropriety of crossing words with her father. It might not be difficult, it might even conceivably be sweet, to suffer for the truth if one could be certain that it *was* the truth. But to suffer and involve others in her suffering for what might only be opinionated error . . . to incur the irrevocable loss of her father's love and risk the terrors of the block for no other end than the final destruction of the hopes to which her mother had so valiantly clung . . . Blindly she groped for enlightenment. There was no longer much use in asking it of God, since it was precisely her ability to comprehend His answer of which she stood in need of reassurance. Still less could she ask it of the one person on earth in whom she longed to place her absolute trust and lay the problem of whether what the King asked her was right before her father. In her desperation she besought Cromwell to grant her an interview and contrived to smuggle out a letter to Chapuys—perhaps before the receipt of the order for her stricter confinement— informing him of her distress and imploring him not to leave her without counsel in her 'extreme necessity'.

Her petition to Cromwell reached a man in the last depths of fear and consternation. He had engaged himself to Henry to gain Mary's submission and failed when he had seemed on the verge of succeeding: Wolsey's fate in like circumstances loomed ominously before him. During the long deliberations of the Council he had been so violently attacked by his enemies for shielding Mary from her just punishment that for four or five days, he told Chapuys, he had looked upon himself as a man lost and dead. Though his reply to Mary's appeal has suffered from fire and time, the panic in which it was written stands out as unmistakably in the mutilated sentences of the original as in the modern reconstruction:

'Madam, I have received yr letters, whereby it appeareth you be in great discomfort, and do desire that I should find the means to speak with you. For answer whereunto, ye shall understand, that how great soever yr discomfort is, it can be no greater than mine, who

hath upon yr letters spoken so much of yr repentance
for yr wilful obstinacy against the K's Highness,
and of yr humble submission in all things, without
exception and disqualification, to obey to his pleasure
and laws, that knowing how diversely and contrarily
you proceeded at the late being of his Maj's counsell
with you, I am much ashamed of that I have said, and
likewise afraid of that I have done; in so much that
the sequel thereof shall be God knoweth. Thus with
yr folly you undo yourself and all that hath wished you
good; and yet I will say unto you, as I said else where
heretofore; that it were a great pity you should not be
an example in a punishment, if ye will make yourself
an example in the contempt of God, your natural
father and his laws, by your own only fantasy, con-
tary to the judgments and determinations of all men,
that you must confess do know and love God as well
as you, except you will show yourself presumption
(uous). Wherefore, Madame, to be plain with you, as
God is my witness, like as I think you the most
obstinate and obdurate woman all things considered
that ever was, and one that so persevering, well
deserveth the rewards of malice in extremity of mischief: so I dare not open my lips to name you, unless
I may have such a ground thereunto, that it may
appear you were mistaken, or at the least that you both
be repentant for your ingratitude and miserable
unkindness, and ready to do all things that ye be
bound unto by yr duty of allegiance, if nature were
secluded from you, and in a like degree planted in the
same, as it is in every other common subject. And
therefore I have sent unto you a certain book of
Articles, whereunto if you will set your name you shall
undoubtedly please God, being the same conformable
to his truth, so as you will in semblable manner conceive it in yr heart without dissimulation. Upon the

receipt whereof again from you, with a letter declaring that you think in your heart that you have subscribed with yr hand, I shall efstoons adventure to speak for your reconciliation. And if you will not with speed leave all your sinister counsells, which have brought you to the point of utter undoing, without remedy, and herein follow mine advice, I take leave of you forever, and desire you never to write or make mean unto me hereafter. For I will never think you other than the most ungrateful, unnatural and most obstinate person living, both to God and yr most dear and benign father. And I advise you to nothing, but I beseech God never to help me, if I know it not so certainly to be yr bounded duty, by God's laws and man's laws, that I must needs judge that person that shall refuse it, not meet to live in a christian congregation; to the witness whereof I take Christ, whose mercy I refuse, if I write anything unto you that I have not professed in my heart, and know to be true.'

The 'certain book of Articles' merely put into formal language the first four of the six questions submitted by Norfolk and his colleagues.

Chapuys' reply came as promptly as Cromwell's. He too, was by now thoroughly frightened, not for himself but his master, with whom he had been in constant communication over the advice to be given Mary in her peril. They were confronted by a most serious dilemma. If Mary acceded to her father's demands she would gravely impair the influence which His Catholic Majesty exercised over the minds of the English people as the result of his identification with Catherine and the Pope's cause. But if she refused and was executed, as Chapuys had come to believe, and led Charles to believe, that she surely would be, the one real hope of restoring and maintaining that influence in the future would have been extinguished. For her to stand firm was from the Imperial point of view important but to continue to live was vital.

The dilemma was reflected in Chapuys' answer. As before, on her removal to Hatfield, he sent her, as he subsequently recounted to the Emperor, 'the form of the protestation she must make apart. I also warned her that she must secure the King's pardon and if possible not give her approval to the said statutes except as she was able to do so agreeably to God and her conscience, or that she should only promise not to infringe the said statutes without expressing approval'. But this was only what Chapuys would have liked but knew after reading Mary's appeal he could not have. Sir Thomas More had taken the line of offering not to infringe the statute without expressing approval and failed to satisfy. So the Ambassador to provide against her suffering the like fate (he is still reporting to the Emperor) went on

'telling her among other things that she must make up her mind, if the King persisted in his obstinacy, or that she found evidence that her life was in danger, either by maltreatment or otherwise, to consent to her father's wish, assuring her that such was your advice, and that to save her life, on which depended the peace of the realm, and the great evils which prevail here, she must do everything and dissemble for some time, as the protestations made and the cruel violence shown her preserved her rights inviolate and likewise her conscience, seeing that nothing was required of her expressly against God or the articles of faith, and God regarded more the intention than the act; and that now she had more occasion to do so than during the life of the Concubine, as it was now proposed to deprive the Bastard and make her heiress; and I felt assured that if she came to court she would by her wisdom set her father again in the right road, to which the inter-

cession of your Majesty through the reconciliation
and establishment of amity would induce.'

Coming from Chapuys, the loyal friend upon whom she
and her mother had been so long accustomed to rely, the
advice could not but have carried weight. But coming,
as he so strongly emphasised, from her cousin, his
Catholic Majesty, the Emperor of the West, the one
living person beside her father for whom she could feel
a reverence and trust amounting to awe, it acted upon
her distraught reasonings like a narcotic, lulling them
into welcome if uneasy rest. In part it corresponded with
what was already in her own mind, the feeling she had
not long since tried to convey to Chapuys when he had
almost arranged for her escape abroad, that it would be
wrong of her to desert her post, that it was perhaps in
God's design to make her the instrument of her father's
redemption from error and the restoration of England
to the unity of Christ. But beyond that, reaching to
the core of the whole question, sapping her whole position,
was the pronouncement, almost certainly unexpected
and utterly numbing from such a source, that 'nothing
was required (of her) expressly against God or the Articles
of Faith.' For this was precisely what her father asked her
to admit and all that he asked her to admit. If the Pope's
authority was not expressly derived from God, as it was
certainly not laid down in the Creeds, what ground had
she for denying the right of 'the mouth of England' to
say in the words of *King John*

> '. . . *that no Italian priest shall tithe*
> *or toil in our dominions.*'

To this question even trained theologians of unimpeachable orthodoxy were having trouble in finding an answer.
The character of Renaissance thought, of the Popes
themselves and their temporal preoccupations, had com-

bined not only to lower esteem for the papacy to something less than it had been in earlier ages or was again
to be, but to encourage doubt whether it was of divine
institution at all. Even Sir Thomas More, who was so
cheerfully to die for differing with Henry on this point,
had once openly questioned whether it was anything more
than a convenient invention for keeping order and discipline in the Church, and so advised Henry when the
latter was earning the title of Defender of the Faith with
his book maintaining the papal claims in their entirety
against Luther. For Mary, beset with the insistence of all
those in authority over her, with neither parent nor
spiritual adviser to consult, the systematic defence of a
doctrine canonically still far from perfected was intellectually impossible; she could only repeat what she had
been taught by teachers now discredited. She could not,
like the contemporary martyrs, invoke her learning or
even, after the answers to her supplications, the common
conscience of Christian mankind. She had taken her
stand on what she had assumed to be a principle of her
faith, and there is no creature more helpless than a
young person who, having taken such a stand, finds on all
authority available that no real principle was involved, at
least none of sufficient importance to be ridiculously
obstinate about. If the Pope was not head of the visible
Church, if in consequence her father and mother had
never been husband and wife, she could no longer even
be sure that she was real, for upon those two pillars of
certainty had the reality of the world and of her own being
in it largely rested. There was nowhere else to turn,
nothing more to say. She signed and returned the document Cromwell had sent her without troubling to read it.

'The confession of me the Lady Marye made upon
certain points and articles under written' contained
nothing new. After asking pardon of the King 'whom I
have obstinately and inobediently offended', she sub-

mitted herself unconditionally 'to his Highness and to all
the singular laws and statutes of this realm, as becometh
a true and faithful subject to do' and swore to 'obey,
keep and maintain them' with all the power, force and
qualities with which God had endowed her while she
lived. She then signed individually the two crucial para-
graphs. In the first, after recognising 'the King's Highness
to be the Supreme Head in earth under Christ of the
Church of England', she utterly rejected the Bishop of
Rome's pretended authority, etc. within the realm and
renounced all right of appeal on any ground whatsoever.
In the second she acknowledged 'that the marriage
heretofore had between his Majesty and my mother, the
late Princess Dowager, was by God's law and man's law
incestuous and unlawful'. If there was nothing new in
the conditions exacted of Mary, the language in which
they were presented indicated the novelty that had of
late entered into human thinking. The bitter conflict
somewhat irrelevantly precipitated by the Reformation
as to whether the Church or the individual was the ultimate judge in matters of conscience had opened the way
for a third party, the secular State, to usurp the claims of
both contestants.

'As soon as the news of her subscription arrived,
incredible joy was shown in all the Court', except by
those who feared that Henry would now turn upon them
for having advocated her death. Henry rejoiced as over a
lost sheep found, a prodigal daughter returned. Cromwell
came riding to Hunsdon with 'a most gracious letter'
which he delivered together with his master's benediction
and his own plea for forgiveness 'kneeling on the ground';
and though the meeting with her father and his new wife
was deferred until she had written another letter expressly
asking for it in the same sickening terms as before, she
was left in no doubt that in that respect as in others she
would shortly be gratified.

Yet her own heart still prevented her sharing completely in the general delight over her escape and the compensations now awaiting her. Though to Chapuys she conveyed the impression that she was 'very happy', he also reported her at the same time to be 'much dejected'. It was perhaps inevitable that a tension so acute and prolonged should be followed by a sense of relief and of depression equally marked . . . Her doubts were not yet at rest; in the circumstances of her capitulation they scarcely could be. Chapuys, realising it, told the Emperor 'that now she has done it, on my assurance that it was the will of your Majesty, it would be a wondrous consolation to know it by letters from you.' He also transmitted at her desire a request to the Pope for absolution in case she had done wrong—unaware of or desperately indifferent to the fact that she was violating her compact with her father and storing up supreme danger if he ever found out. Paul III, more alert to the danger than she, refused the special dispensation asked for but allowed her the benefit of a general instruction to confessors permitting them to absolve from the 'new English errors' those who upon examination could show satisfactory cause. What thereafter happened between Mary and her spiritual advisers can, of course, never be known.

To say that the years just past were critical for Mary seems a truism almost too obvious. Yet it is true in no obvious sense. The years between 16 and 20 are critical in every young life, even the most commonplace. In hers they began in loneliness and dread, moved in a crescendo of ill-treatment to a sustained climax of bewilderment and terror, and ended in her utter abasement. It is but natural to assume that an ordeal so extraordinary must have had consequences proportionate to itself. If it did, they are not perceptible. Neither in act nor word did the experience of those years betray its influence on her later life. True, Francis I presently instructed his ambassador

to ascertain from her physician 'whether all she had suffered would not prevent her bearing children', but of
any link between the ordeal of her youth and the tragedy
of her middle age there is no evidence whatsoever. Her
father set out to break her spirit and he broke it; there is
no way of estimating to what extent if any a broken spirit
differs after time's repair from what it might have been.
Even upon her external fortunes the terms of surrender
wrung from her made no visible difference. Had she
failed to resist, or resisted successfully, the result could
not have been other than it was. She would have been
Queen of England just the same, her title no worse and
no better, and gone down to posterity in the pages of
John Foxe as Bloody Mary with just as much or little
justification.

But the measure of a crisis is not necessarily in the
traces it leaves. A crisis is a matter of choices rather than
of their consequences and the course chosen may leave
none upon the plane of appearances—of events, that is,
as they actually occurred—whereas the course rejected
might have affected it beyond all recognition. The reason
and the imagination have their own sphere of action no
less than the brute chaos of events; to hold that what
did not happen can never possess the meaning and importance of what did is to deny them their prime function
of assessing the actual in terms of the possible, giving to
each its due and valid significance, and relegate literature,
philosophy and science to the status of mere excrescences
upon reality.

Instead of resisting and submitting, Mary might to
the end have refused to submit, as she came so near to
doing . . . and then her choice, instead of changing
nothing, would have changed everything. Either she
would have been put to death at once as she expected or
if not, in all probability when the North rose three months
later in the Pilgrimage of Grace and placed at the fore-

front of its demands her restoration together with that of the old order of things for which she stood. And in that event not only would the history of England have had to be rewritten, but something new and glorious added to the human story yet to be written—the tale (perhaps told in some poet's tragic masterpiece or possibly even in articles of canonisation) of the King's daughter who, like Antigone and Joan of Arc, laid down her life for what she believed. It was so near a thing, so small a particle of decision that withdrew her from inscription upon the golden calendar of heroes and saints. No lack of courage debarred her, nor any fear of death, for which she often prayed as a blessed deliverance. With all the necessary desire, even eagerness, to obey her Lord's injunction and persevere to the end, she lost her way before the end and fell into a mental confusion which permitted the phantasms of conflicting doubts, duties and loyalties to blur her own unique vision of the truth. But it is precisely the mental clarity she lost that is the particular distinguishing grace of saints and heroes in their supreme hour of crisis.

CHAPTER FIVE

An Interval of Quiet

The closing scene in the drama, Mary's reconciliation with her father, was not long delayed, though its circumstances are not clear. Two letters from Chapuys indicate that it took place on 26th July, three weeks after her 'confession', with a visit from Henry and Jane, who brought not only kind words but gifts, Jane a diamond ring and Henry a thousand crowns for pocket money with the hearty (though not altogether accurate) assurance that there was plenty more where that came from. Chapuys later admitted that his report was based on hearsay and that 'mixed with the sweet food of paternal kindness were a few drams of gall and bitterness', but that the meeting took place when he said seems certain from the entry for that date in the diary of Thomas Wriothesley, later Lord Chancellor and Earl of Southampton, who recorded that 'the Lady Mary, daughter to the King by Queen Catherine, was brought riding from Hunsdon secretly in the night to Hackney and (that) afternoon the King and Queen came thither and there the King spake with his dear and well-beloved daughter Mary, which had not spoken with the King her father in five years before, and there she remained till Friday (the next day) at night, and then she rode to Hunsdon again secretly.'

The secrecy was doubtless imposed by Henry in order to enable him to judge for himself the sincerity of his daughter's submission before admitting her again to court. Perhaps he was not altogether satisfied, as Chapuys intimates, since there is no mention of her return to public life before a number of months had elapsed. One account, contained in a manuscript of somewhat later date, describes it in the following manner:

'. . . Upon a time as the King and Queen were together, she being great with child with King (sic) Edward, the King said unto her, "Why, darling, how happeneth you are no merrier?"

She wisely answered, "Now it hath pleased your Grace to make me your wife, there are none but my inferiors to make merry withall, your Grace excepted, unless it would please you that we might enjoy the company of the Lady Mary's Grace at the court; I could be merry with her."

"We will have her here, darling, if she will make thee merry."

So presently the King commanded all her women to be put to her again, and all in rich array with his daughter, the Lady Mary, in most gorgeous apparel, to come the next day unto the court, all apparelled at the King's charge. The King and Queen standing in the chamber of presence by the fire. This worthy lady entered with all her train. So soon as she came within the chamber door she made low courtesy unto him; in the midst of the chamber she did so again, and when she came to him, she made them both low curtsey, and falling on her knees asked his blessing, who after he had given her his blessing, took her up by the hand and kissed her, and the Queen also, both bidding her welcome. Then the King, turning him to the lords there in presence, said, "Some of you were desirous that I should put this jewel to death."

"That had been great pity," quote the Queen, "to have lost your chiefest jewel of England."

But Mary, knowing that when her father flattered,

most mischief was likely to ensue, her colour coming and going, at last in a swoon fell down amongst them. With that the King, being greatly perplexed, what for the fear of his daughter, and the frighting of his wife that was then great with child, sought all means possible to revive her, and being come to herself, bid her be of good comfort, for nothing should go against her, and after perfect recovery, took her by the hand and walked up and down with her. Then commandment was made that she should be called Lady Princess and the other Lady Elizabeth. "Why, governor," quoth the Lady Elizabeth, being but a child, (3 in fact) "how happs it yesterday Lady Princess and to-day but Lady Elizabeth." Here was a haughty stomach be-times.'

The story has its charms, even though strict truth is not amongst them; probably, like many others, it was invented, in part at least, to amplify the early biography of Queen Elizabeth, whose 'haughty stomach' at a most tender age it certainly illustrates. But apart from the fact that Mary was never styled Lady Princess, Jane could not have been great with the future King Edward before the spring of 1537, and Wriothesley had already noted, on 22nd December, 1536, how after the knighting of the Lord Mayor in the Presence Chamber at Westminster 'the King's Grace, the Queen's Grace and my Lady Mary . . . took their horses at the said palace of Westminster accompanied with a goodly company of lords, ladies and gentlemen' and rode through the icy streets of London to Greenwich—they could not go by boat since the Thames was frozen solid—through files of 'friars standing in Fleet Street in copes of gold with crosses and candlesticks and censers', past the whole choir of St. Paul's singing and censing at the west door of the Cathedral and 'all the crafts of the City standing in their best liveries with hoods on their shoulders, which was a goodly sight to behold.'

There followed for Mary a comparatively uneventful interval of ten years until her father's death. Whatever doubts he may still have entertained of her appear soon to have been set at rest. With the collapse of the Pilgrimage of Grace, which occurred at about the time that Wriothesley reports her reappearance at court, her power for harm was very considerably reduced, while her conduct plainly showed her anxiety to avoid every possible cause of suspicion. After having foresworn her allegiance to the See of Peter and to the memory of her mother, she raised no objections to taking her opinion of 'pilgrimages, purgatory, relicks and such like' from 'the King's Highness, my most benign father' and adapted herself to Henry's various exercises in ecclesiastical improvement without protest. One lesson she had learned, the one which every Tudor had sooner or later to learn, to say nothing about matters concerning which she could do nothing. With impassive face she took up her position at the King's side, to greet distinguished visitors when summoned to do so or rode behind him in the innumerable public processions dedicated to public rejoicing or sorrow—weddings, coronations, baptisms, funerals and the like—so many of them occasioned by his persistence in marrying; with tight lips she managed to hear the oft-repeated tidings of the butchery of those dear to her and silently lock away in some inaccessible recess of herself the memory of a soft breast against which she had often rested her head in some desolate moment of childhood or of a kind, patient voice correcting her youthful errors of syntax or of another gently admonishing her in confession. Publicly her life during that interval was pretty much that of a figure in an intermittent pageant. Privately it may have been full enough, with her studies, her recreations and the many small human relations inevitably incurred by one of her rank, but what was really going on inside her it is almost impossible to say, since nothing happened of a nature to bring or force it out.

A great deal of her time in those years was given to her studies, which she resumed and expanded with ardour. If her mind was not primarily a scholar's, it unquestionably possessed considerable powers of curiosity and application. From the classics and history she branched out on her own—at least it is reasonable so to infer from the absence of any named masters—into astronomy, geography, physics and mathematics. A French visitor of the period, impressed with the variety and intensity of her routine, tried to describe it for her fellow countrymen in verse:

> *Souvent vaquet aux divines leçons,*
> *Souvent cherchoit des instruments les sons,*
> *Ou s'occupoit a faire quelque ouvrage,*
> *Ou apprenoit quelqu'estrange langage.*
>
> *Puis a savoir raison des mouvemens,*
> *Et le secret de tout le firmament;*
> *Du monde aussi la situation,*
> *Des elemens l'association;*
> *Puis sagement avec mathematique*
> *Meloit raison, moral, politique.*
> *Puis apprenoit Latine et Grecque, lettre,*
> *Par oraison, par histoire, et par metre . . .*

From the whole poem one gathers that her working day was divided between her reading of Scripture, her study of foreign languages and classical literature and history, the sciences and philosophy both political and moral, original compositions and the 'lighter employment of working' such as needlework and music. Various of her original compositions survive, including three prayers in

Latin entitled 'A Meditation Touching Adversity', 'Against the Assault of Vices', and a 'Prayer to be Used at the Hour of Death'; all are competent in the expression of their thought but without any striking originality. She also contributed, a little later, to a translation of Erasmus's Paraphrase on the Gospel of St. John which gained current celebrity. A literary effort in a lighter vein, alluded to by Cromwell in a note, 'Item, to remember the Balade made of the Prynces by my Lady Mary' is unfortunately not extant. One would like a specimen of her own contribution to the game of versified trifling in which throughout her life she derived such huge enjoyment from the proficiency of others.

For she was no mere blue-stocking. Even after all that she had been through she remained what she had been brought up to be, an all-round Renaissance woman. Putting aside her book or her music, she threw herself with equal zest into the antics of tumblers and jesters no less than the epigrammatic crackle of the professional wits, into dancing, masques, gambling, gossip, dressing up and, despite the handicap of her size and frequent illnesses, the most strenuous of sports. Scope was given her for all of these activities when a new household, numbering forty-two persons, was allotted to her, and an allowance made her of £40 a quarter, to which Henry added further sums at Christmas, when her expenses ran particularly high, and irregularly on other occasions. It was then that she began to keep the scrupulous private accounts which afford the best insight as to how she passed her time in those years. They show that she had not only to bear the cost of the transport of her suite from place to place and of repairs to the various houses in which she lived, but to pay for her own clothes, recreations and medical services and to distribute alms, tips and presents on a scale quite out of proportion to her means. Her rank assured that the calls on her would be unending while her own nature forbade her to be parsimonious.

Thus through her accounts run items, repeated over and over in one form or another, like 'given to the prison houses of London . . .xxs', 'To a poor man towards his marriage at the request of Mr. Tyrell . . . ½ angel' (3/9) to another poor man come to solicit a gift for his ailing child 15/-, to still a third 'who desired my Lady's Grace to have christened his child . . .xs'. This last type of appeal was incessant and one which she seemed unable to refuse. All sorts and conditions of people, from the neighbouring woodcutter or her own stableman to the heads of the nobility desired her to stand godmother to their children, just as so many of the rich and great applied to place their daughters in her service, for she represented a particular quality in England, as had her mother before her, of instructed piety and decency which even the new style of gentry who had began to neglect them in their own lives would have been glad to secure for their children; but with only four 'gentlewomen allotted to her household, at a salary of £10 a year apiece,' Mary could without offence restrict the offices of intimacy to a few chosen, some of them, like Susan Clarence, Margaret Baynton and Jane Dormer, almost life-long friends. It was they who accompanied her to christenings, attended her on private and public visits, enjoyed with her evenings of music of their own and others' making '(given to my Lord Marquess's servant for singing' 8/6, etc.) gathered round to criticise 'George Mountjoy's drawing of my Lady's Grace to his Valentine' (price 40/-), helped her to cut and sew the gay costumes one could almost reconstruct from the several entries like 'Paid to the gold-drawer for pipes and pearls for a gown li.vii.xvs' and worked with her in preparing the gifts whose delivery at each year's end sent her servants scurrying far and wide.

Indeed a cursory examination of her accounts might

easily give the impression that most of her income and a considerable proportion of her time between one New Year's Day and the next went to the planning and purchase or making of the presents which she so freely distributed to friends, relatives, members of her father's court, her godchildren, dependents and constantly enlarging circle of acquaintance. Sometimes they were simply ordered wholesale—'paid for vi bonnets bought of my Lady Mayoress of London, vi Li (£)' but more often they were selected singly after much consideration and looking about, and frequently they consisted of the work of her own hands: bits of furniture which she restored and embellished or articles of household use or personal wear deftly sewn and embroidered. Many if not most of these were destined for the members of what might be called her immediate family if that be taken to comprise not only her father, sister and brother (the son, Edward, born to Jane in October 1537) but her various stepmothers. With all these last except Catherine Howard, who worsted her in a short-lived tiff over some matter of precedence, she was on excellent terms and remained so with the two who survived Henry, Anne of Cleves and Catherine Parr, to the end of their lives, continuing to visit the one in her retirement after Henry had put her away and receiving much kindness and encouragement in her literary efforts from the other after his death and before her unfortunate remarriage to Thomas Seymour. The account books for some three years between 1539 and 1542 within which all the brief married lives of Anne of Cleves and Catherine Howard fell, are missing, but thereafter, from the dispatch of a head-dress for Anne and a cushion worked to pattern for Catherine Parr, no New Year's Day passed without some item for each on which thought and care as well as money had been spent.

With Elizabeth and Edward her relations were to all

appearances those to be expected between an adult sister and her juniors still in the nursery. Elizabeth she continued to call 'sister' as she had promised, even though she may already have felt the doubt which she expressed later as to whether the girl was in fact Henry's; certainly at this stage she showed no resentment against her on her mother's account by word or act. 'My sister Elizabeth,' she reported to Henry in the course of a holiday spent with the younger child, 'is in good health and, thanks be to our Lord, such a child toward as I doubt not your Highness shall have cause to rejoice of in time coming.' Certainly at this time, and for several years after Anne Boleyn's execution, Henry did little rejoicing over his younger daughter but grossly neglected her, as Lady Brian's well-known letter to the Privy Council pleading for the means with which properly to clothe and feed her attests. Within her small capacity Mary did her best to make amends. The paths of the two crossed fairly frequently as they moved from house to house and the elder would provide various diversions for the younger, such as sending for Edward's company of minstrels to come and play for them; or, noting the state of the girl's wardrobe, present her with a kirtle of yellow satin, one of the articles of which Lady Brian reported her to stand in need. Twice at short intervals the accounts record the dispatch out of Mary's none too ample funds of a pound for extra spending money. How Elizabeth, the most self-contained if now and then forward-spoken of small girls, responded it is not possible to say. The regular remembrances sent to Mary at the New Year, such as the 'little chain and pair of hose, silk and gold', were unlikely as yet to represent her own active sentiments.

Whatever element of will, of a determination to suspend her doubts and memories and be kind because it was the right thing to do, may have governed Mary's attitude towards Anne Boleyn's daughter, there was plainly none because none was needed in her conduct toward Jane Seymour's son. Jane had been uniformly good to her; as soon as Mary was in a position to respond a mutual fondness, pleasant and easy, had grown up between them, and Jane's death twelve days after giving birth to Edward had been a grievous loss to Mary. Henry, who for once seems himself to have been sincerely stricken, gave her the place of Chief Mourner at the great funeral which culminated in St. George's Chapel at Windsor. He also appointed her to be godmother to Edward at his christening, comfortably unaware that he was entrusting to the most uncompromising of English queens the sponsorship in Christ of the first of England's Protestant kings. Her delight in the little prince was only less rapturous than Henry's own—in part, perhaps, because the long-delayed heir removed the principal cause of constraint between them, but also because the child itself aroused in her an affection which, as reflected in her reports of him to Henry, might at times forgivably be mistaken for a doting maiden aunt's. As his first New Year's gift she sent him a jewelled cap at the extravagant price of 45/——with which may be compared the 12/- she spent on silver with which to decorate a box for Elizabeth on the same occasion. Two years later, when she sent Elizabeth the kirtle of yellow satin, she worked for Edward a little coat of crimson in the same material. Soon he began to learn his letters, and his elder sister, who spared herself neither trouble nor expense to visit him, was able to add to her descriptions of his delicate prettiness and fetching sobriety (for which he was distinguished even by the standard of Tudor young) her breathless astonishment at his cleverness. When he was 5 she recognised his altered status by giving him 'a Boke lymmed with gold' of which the binding alone cost her 29/-. Edward in his serious young way reciprocated her devotion. Amongst his first writings were his declaration of love to her in Latin—'*Amo te sicut frater debet amare carissimam sororem . . .*', '*Valetudo tua laetificat me, quia te amo, et aegritudo tue facit me tristem*'. Odd as it now seems, she was the gay sister in whose capacity for fun and taste in bright clothes he took pleasure, Elizabeth the grave one like himself, 'my sweet sister Temperance', and there can be no doubt that she remained his favourite of the two even after the Puritans got hold of him and caused him to deplore the 'foreign dances and merriments' to which his 'dear sister Mary' was given as 'enchantments of the evil one' and unbecoming to 'a most Christian princess'.

Generous herself, she begot generosity in others. The giving of presents was not a one-way traffic; each New Year's Day there poured in on her from far and near gifts representing a discriminating adjustment between the donor's means and degree of familiarity on the one hand and her status and needs on the other: useful sums of money from her father (though occasionally from others), a standing gilt cup from her brother, a length of Spanish silk from Anne of Cleves, a nightgown and £25 from Catherine Parr and from outside the family circle a wide variety of objects both similar and dissimilar, from greyhounds for coursing to a swan or exotic garden produce like strawberries or artichokes for her table. Policy as well as generosity added to her store. The first horse she had been allowed to own, or indeed to mount, for a long time came to her from Cromwell soon after her reconciliation with her father, and the letter she wrote in return describing the pleasure and benefit she derived and her own and her groom's pride in the animal's mettle was doubtless as welcome to the giver as the gift was to the receiver. Many others as well now thought it politic to recall themselves to her notice. But many more, from amongst the humble who had at every opportunity cheered and unceasingly prayed for her, were now able to make their little offerings of a cake, a cheese, a basket of eggs or apples, a bunch of roses or a pheasant, the legal title to which it might have been ungracious to inquire into. All had their reward, the poor bringing their tribute in person and the servants delivering it for their masters, since it would have been unseemly for a royal lady to send away any bringer of gifts empty-handed. To a 'poor woman bringing apples' would go a shilling, to another 'for bringing unto my Lady's Grace bacon and eggs' twenty pence, up to 22/6 to Cromwell's liveried emissary for delivering a New Year's gift and 35/- to a gentleman of the Lord Admiral's for bringing a coffer with ten pairs of Spanish gloves from a Duchess in Spain.

Two other forms of expenditure help to explain why she could never make ends meet and was driven to asking her father through Cromwell either for additional sums or an increase in her allowance; it was clearly a task she did not relish—'And thus, my lord,' ends one such appeal, 'I am ashamed always to be a beggar unto you, but that the occasion is such that at this time I cannot choose'—but yet could hardly avoid with a deficit in her quarterly balance amounting at times to £60 or 150% of her stipend; usually Henry sent the extra sums and after six years increased her allowance. The first of the two so to speak unproductive charges upon it, in that they brought no tangible return like giving presents, was her frequent and heavy outlay for medical attendance. Over and over, occasionally twice a month or even oftener, the neat figures in the account books record payments to one surgeon or another of 20/- (later raised to 22/6) for bleeding, 20/- to the apothecary for a visit and 7/6 to his assistant for bringing potions or ointments, and now and then an odd sum like the 45/- to Nicholas Simpson sent by the King from London to draw her tooth. How she managed to support the loss of the blood they extracted from her and the witches' brews they poured into her and still dash flushed and happy after the hounds or dance a long evening through seems inexplicable except on the theory of a constitution and temperament subject to excessive variations from the normal equilibrium—a theory which if sound would explain much about her.

So also, perhaps, does a fact which would appear to fit in with it, an addiction to gambling that vied with her love of sport and dancing. It was a passion she inherited from her father who, after devoting whole nights to it in his youth, had given it up only to return to it in middle age and lose the bells and leads of an expropriated abbey to a crony at a sitting. Mary seems to have been no luckier a player than Henry. Sitting down with 45/-, which she generally allowed herself for an evening's play, she had next day to confess to the keeper of her accounts a debt 'to my Lady Carew lent her grace at cards . . . xxxs', similar sums at different times to others and once as much as the whole of her original stake borrowed from Mr. Wriothesley. Nor was it only at cards that she lost her money, for she was equally ready to bet 'a frontlet lost in a wager to my Lady Margaret', her Scottish cousin, or 'a breakfast at a game of bowls'.

Yet, despite all her manifold activities, one retains an impression of deadness in surveying those years; perhaps because they appeared to be leading nowhere except a dead end. She duly made her appearance as the first lady in England at the reception to Anne of Cleves or the funeral of Jane Seymour and on other occasions of state as the first lady after whoever happened for the time being to be Queen; but first or second, she was little more than a decorative supernumerary. If regarded as heiress-presumptive to the Crown—and it seemed to matter little whether she was so regarded after Edward's birth—she

was admitted to no closer concern with the Crown's
business than if she had been a private person. But if
regarded as a private person, there was also a pointless-
ness to her existence, since no particular attention seems
to have been given to her future either by others or herself. The natural prospect for a young woman of her age
would have been marriage, but though bridegrooms
were put forward—amongst them at one time Cromwell—
and one suitor came from Germany to pay his court
in person, it is impossible to believe that any of them
were considered seriously. Henry's policy shifted from
right to left and back again, from the Ten Articles to
exploratory conversations with the Lutherans, from the
Six Articles ('the whip of six strings') to a temporary
accommodation with the forces of reform of which Anne
of Cleves was the unluckily-selected token; the character
of Mary's suitors followed closely upon these veerings,
changing and disappearing with them. Nor did she herself show much interest, professing herself ready to
accept her father's choice but by her own preferring to
remain single.

What she awaited of the future it is impossible to say.
That she expected ever to reign seems unlikely: her
pleasure in Edward's birth seems altogether sincere,
and like most people she doubtless expected him to
outgrow his early ailments, in due course marry, have
children and reign in her father's stead. All that she
apparently asked of life was to be left in peace with her
studies, her devotions and her friends, to perform her
works of charity and make of her household, 'to which the
greatest lords were suitors to place their daughters in
her service' something like 'a true school of virtuous
demeanour'. She enjoyed receiving and talking with
foreigners, but when Henry became suspicious that too
many were seeking her company, she agreed to put an
end to their coming without demur. With no power to

affect, and outwardly unaffected by, the fierce violence of these latter years of Henry's reign, she might almost have been living in a cloister had there been such a thing left in England. Her old promise to Cromwell to be his 'humble petitioner . . . in like case' remained perforce ignored as his enemies closed in and hustled him from the apex of his glory to the block. No sound was heard from her during the holocaust that in its course swept away so many who had befriended her at grave risk, Poles, Courtenays and Carews, and came to its end with the hacking to pieces by an inexpert executioner of the 80-year-old Countess of Salisbury, the woman she had loved most after her mother; though afterwards she was reported to be so 'very ill' as to be in some danger of her life. It was as if her father (who on this occasion showed serious concern at her symptoms) had really injured something vital in her beyond repair while he lived.

CHAPTER SIX

Henry's Legacy

Henry died in the early morning of 28th January, 1547. Though only 55, he was not taken unawares: and as his body, swollen and suppurating with disease, lapsed into immobility, he gave final form to his will and delivered it to Parliament for enactment into law. It assumed without need of specific declaration that if his son survived he would succeed him, in fulfilment of the main purpose of his life's striving. But the striving had also entailed the further consequence that if the son, a small boy in precarious health, failed to reach maturity, the Crown would be left without an appointed wearer. Little as he fancied a female succession, an open one held prospect of such supreme disaster that Henry consented to embrace the alternative he had been trying for twenty years to avoid and authorised nature to resume her normal course. In the event of Edward dying without issue he was to be followed by Mary, and she in like event by Elizabeth; though for fear of appearing to admit possible error in the dissolution of his first two marriages, both daughters continued to bear the stain of illegitimacy imputed to them previously. Should Elizabeth in her turn die childless, the will directed that the descendants of his elder sister Margaret, late Queen of Scotland, should be passed over in favour of those of the younger, Mary, Duchess of Suffolk, mainly for the reason that the representative of the elder line, the infant Queen of Scots, was a foreigner and, as a protégée of France, a potential enemy. Evidently Henry did not mean nature to have it all her own way, though in requiring her to fit two declared bastards and a junior branch in place of a senior into the order of succession, he seems to have overtaxed her powers of accommodation, as subsequent test was to prove.

So Mary received back her birthright, in fact if not completely in form. The taint left upon it precluded her from resuming the title of Princess, so that she was still only the Lady Mary, and the financial provision made for her, though not ungenerous, could be presumed to reflect the difference. But for her these were trifles of which even to take notice would have been an impiety towards the gift and the giver, all the more so in view of the language of fatherly tenderness in which he conveyed it. Atonement had been made, the pledge of mutual love and confidence irrevocably sealed: a consummation so perfect that the document which recorded it carried its own warranty to be the last word in human wisdom, her infallible guide through whatever troubles and per-lexities it might give rise to.

Time and peace were given her to assimilate her altered condition. Except for her private sorrow and the long-drawn solemnities of public mourning, Henry's death transformed the perspective of her existence with-out disturbing its tranquil routine. As second person in the kingdom, lawful as well as rightful heiress to a sickly boy of 9, her prestige and political importance were vast yet of such a nature as to place her outside, in a sense above, politics. Her income, some £3,500 a year in lands, was sufficient to maintain her station in modest dignity, and as her own mistress, deferring neither to ministers nor stepmothers whether hostile or friendly, she was free to conduct her life in her own chosen way. Except on special occasions of duty, London rarely saw her; a choice partly dictated by her health, which at intervals so troubled her that she herself had little expectation of

outliving the King her brother. Following her inclina-
tions and the indications of the seasons, she divided her
year between the various properties in Hertfordshire,
Essex and Norfolk settled on her by her father, and
apportioned her days amongst her studies, her good works
and her recreations much as before.

It was a quiet round but a full one. If her friendships
were few they were, as events proved, strong enough
to last out her life, and though most of them throve
within the circle of her household, a number had to be
kept in remembrance, as well as a great deal of business
transacted, by letters passing to and from the outside
world. And if anything was still lacking, whether to occupy
time or fill such void as she might feel from the want of
father and mother or of normal fulfilment in husband
and children, there were the rhythmic cycle of the Offices
and the unceasing Presence on the altar near at hand in
the adjacent oratory to supply it.

While these spiritual comforts remained secure, her
relations with the Council of Regents appointed to
govern during her brother's minority were conducted
with correctness and, in individual instances, cordiality
on both sides. Such relations had largely to do with the
economy of her household, over which they, in their
joint capacity of ministers to Edward VI and executors
of Henry's will, possessed certain rights of supervision.
'The establishment and good ordinance made for the
good rule of the household of the Right Honourable
and most excellent Princess the Lady Mary's Grace,
Sister unto the King's Majesty, at her place in Kenninghall . . .' One of the chaplains was always to be in readiness
to conduct the appropriate services; the clerk of the
closet was to ring the bell at places convenient for summoning the countryside to Matins, Mass and Evensong;
no member of the household might fail in attendance
except for good excuse . . . The emphasis laid on the

strict order of religious observance sounds sadly ironical
in view of what was so soon to follow. All persons entering
the Princess's service were to take an oath of fidelity,
to have their wages declared to them beforehand—
doubtless a necessary provision in a time when pay in
any public or quasi-public establishment was uncertain
and subject to endless bickering—and to give six months'
notice before leaving. Such of the household as were
permitted servants of their own were to engage only
cleanly young men 18 years of age or over, whose hours
of duty were to begin at 7 a.m. in the summer and 8 a.m.
in the winter, and whose conditions of labour precluded
brawling, chiding, swearing or other bad language,
and gaming with dice or otherwise except during the
festive period between Christmas and Twelfth Night.

To these regulations Mary was free to add others at
her discretion, such as 'the ordinances established and
devised by the Lady Mary's grace for the good laudable
order and rule of her stable' where everything from the
care of horses and harness to the high ceremonial of
mounting and attending her on progress are set forth in
punctilious detail. Otherwise the government as such
touched her life but little—so little that when she presently incurred its hostility its only effective way of
striking at her lay through her household. Such contacts
as she had with its members individually were, until
politics intervened, mainly in the form of friendly trans-
actions for the favouring of persons or the transfer of
lands. Politics hardly entered in because for Mary they
consisted, and for the government at this stage they
appeared to consist in keeping things pretty much as
Henry had left them.

One change in his arrangements the Council did in
fact venture to make, but with a view rather to filling an
evident want than to proclaiming a departure in policy.
The art of personal government as practised by the

Tudors consisted largely in maintaining an equilibrium of forces which the monarch could regulate at his discretion, now favouring one faction or grouping of opinion, now another when its aims happened usefully to coincide with his own, but never allowing any completely to dominate the others lest it should succeed in dominating him. Through every fluctuation of policy Henry had retained in his councils exponents of the alternative policy, with each new expedient he had encouraged in those who opposed it the hope that it was that and no more. This formula he followed in his will; to impart stability to the beginning of his son's reign, he carried forward the balance as it stood at the end of his own. Of the Regents there named some inclined to the old faith, more to one of the varieties of the new, the rest to any or none. To emphasise the purely provisional character of whatever ascendancy some might succeed in gaining over the others, the right was reserved to Edward of reviewing any act done in his name when he reached his majority. But a system of government so long submissive to the rule of one was at once seen to be unworkable by the equal collaboration of sixteen. The attempt was therefore abandoned and the sixteen consented, after awarding themselves suitable compensation in properties and peerages, to one of their number, Edward Seymour, Earl of Hertford, the young King's maternal uncle, assuming the rôle of acting monarch under the style of Protector.

The change excited little opposition, either on the country's part or Mary's. To all it was obvious that only in some such way could the collapse of authority dreaded on Henry's death be averted, and no alternative to Seymour was remotely practicable. As the King's nearest male relative he enjoyed a prestige, and as Henry's most successful soldier a popularity, unapproached by any other subject. Moreover, though greedy, like all of Henry VIII's newly-raised favourites, where his own interests were concerned, in public affairs he had a name for moderation which encouraged those who feared the Protestant company he kept to account him a restraining influence upon excessive zeal. In this judgment Mary apparently concurred, as shown by her subsequent disillusion. She had other, more personal reasons as well for feeling amiably disposed towards him: the kindness she had received from his sister, the late Queen Jane, and the affection she felt for his wife, to which she gave testimony in letters addressed to 'my good Nan' or 'my good Gossip'* which remain amongst the few informal relics of her friendships.

The tone and something of the substance of her intercourse with her brother's ministers at this period are conveyed by three specimens of her correspondence. In the first she asks, in the second refuses, a favour, but in both speaking as the Princess elevated above the need to ingratiate or expatiate, or indeed above any need but that of instinctive courtesy. The first, to William Lord Paget, Comptroller of the King's Household and one of the three or four most important men in the government, runs:

'Good Mr. Comptroller,

For so much as my lord protector, and others of the council, promised me heretofore two knights rooms in Windsor; the one to take place presently there, and the other at the next avoidance, I shall most heartily require you to help that George Brygus, this bearer's husband, may now be placed there and have the fee thereof accordingly. In doing whereof, you shall do unto me much pleasure, which, with your other gentleness showed to me in times past, I trust to thank you for at our next meeting.

* A mode of address used between joint god-mothers of the same infant.

And thus, for lack of leisure at this present, I will bid you farewell with my hearty commendations both to yourself and your good wife.

Scribbled at Beaulieu, the 17th of October,
> Your assured friend to my power,
> Marye.'

The second letter is of considerably greater interest. It was addressed to the Protector's younger brother Thomas, Lord Admiral of England, who had written requesting her approval of his matrimonial intentions towards Henry's widow Catherine Parr—an engagement which he had, in fact, already secretly contracted after having proposed in rapid succession for Mary herself and the 13-year-old Elizabeth.

'My Lord,
After my hearty commendations, these shall be to declare that according to your accustomed gentleness, I have received six warrants from you by your servant this bearer, for the which I do give my hearty thanks, by whom also I have received your letter wherein (as methinketh) I perceive strange news, concerning a suit you have in hand to the Queen for marriage, for the sooner obtaining whereof, you seem to think that my letters might do you pleasure. My lord, in this case I trust your wisdom doth consider that if it were for my nearest kinsman and dearest friend alive, of all other creatures in the world it standeth least with my poor honour to be a meddler in this matter, considering whose wife her grace was of late, and besides that, if she be minded to grant your suit, my letters shall do you but small pleasure. On the other side, if the remembrance of the King's Majesty my father (whose soul God pardon) will not suffer her to grant your suit, I am nothing able to persuade her to forget the loss of him, who is as yet very ripe in mine own

remembrance. Wherefore I shall most earnestly require you (the premises considered) to think none unkindness in me, though I refuse to be a meddler any ways in this matter, assuring you that (wooing matters set apart, wherein I, being a maid, am nothing cunning) if otherwise it shall lie in my little power to do you pleasure I shall be as glad to do it as you to require it, both for his blood's sake that you be of, and also the gentleness which I have always found in you. As knoweth Almighty God, to whose tuition I commit you.

From Wanstead, this Saturday at night, being the 4th June.

Your assured friend to my power,
Marye.'

It is hard to see how in the circumstances the letter could have been improved upon. Like one of her mother's, it said precisely what it meant to say, with delicacy yet without circumlocution. Unfortunately it was wasted upon Seymour, who married his Catherine only to lose her in childbirth but continued to pay his addresses to Elizabeth, whom he involved in a grave personal scandal as well as the suspicion of being party to a plot against the State which brought him to the block.

The third letter, though much the same in time, is very different in temper. The tone is set by the topic: one no longer confined within the limits of friendly private adjustment but embracing the whole welfare of the kingdom of which the writer is the potential and the receiver the provisional head. Faced with a resumption of the religious strife which Henry had subdued with iron constraint, the Protector had sought to allay it by relaxing the constraint. The results were disappointing: the sects, instead of being lulled into amity, merely rose to a shriller proficiency of abuse. Legally Henry's settlement still remained in force; Edward's first Paliament did not meet until the tenth month of the reign and fourteen more would elapse before the religion of England was re-defined by law. But from the very beginning the radical Reformers, in the midst and as a part of their struggle for such a redefinition, had succeeded where they were in sufficient strength in suppressing or disallowing Catholic practices until then no less lawful than venerated. Here and there, even before Parliament gave its confirmation, sacred images, painting and stained glass, branded as 'worshipping of stocks and stones', forcibly disappeared from churches and chapels, consecrated beads, bells, bread, water, palms, candles were lumped together with pilgrimages and prayers for the dead as 'papistical superstitions' to be summarily disallowed.

Resentments flared up, local retaliations occurred. But even this was not the worst. To lawless act was joined a licence of language even more frightening and injurious to the ordinary individual. The treatment accorded the cherished and familiar incidentals of worship might wound and sadden him, but the words applied to the sacrifice of the Mass, the fundamental operation of His faith, were an insult to God, a contemptuous rejec-tion of the means He had offered for redemption and entry into eternal life. Hocus-Pocus the scoffers called it, and upon the Eucharist—the adored presence, for Anglican and Roman alike, of the living Christ—loudly lavished such epithets as Jack-in-the-Box, Round Robin, Sacrament of the Halter, etc. The giddier sort en-deavoured, after the manner of their kind in all revolu-tionary manifestations, to translate the words into appro-priate action. In London a priest was murderously assaulted while performing the Consecration, a dead cat, tonsured and robed, nailed up with the Host in its paws to simulate the Elevation. Elsewhere as well such acts of cruelty and blasphemy were perpetrated as almost to confound the call to prayer with the signal for riot.

The government, far from suppressing the militants however tasteless and deliberately provocative their conduct, maintained a discreet if not actually benevolent detachment, the world of contemporary intellectual fashion egged them on with its applause. To so promising a missionary field were soon drawn various distinguished professors of the newer theologies from Germany, Poland and Switzerland to fill prominent pulpits and chairs of divinity in the universities and swell the growing uproar with their assorted accents. Almost the only important voice raised in disapproval from the Protestant side was that of Bishop Ridley deploring the attacks upon the Mass. Such opposition as might have been offered by the spokesmen for orthodoxy had been largely silenced or enfeebled. The leader of the conservative nobility, the Duke of Norfolk, was in the Tower in consequence of an intrigue which had brought his son, the Earl of Surrey, to the block shortly before Henry's death and would have brought him there too had Henry survived a few hours longer; the Catholic Lord Chancellor, the Earl of Southampton, had early been removed from Edward's Council on a charge of the misuse of his office; while from the bench of bishops there temporarily disappeared those two stalwart pillars of the Henrician establishment, Gardiner of Winchester and Bonner of London, to serve cautionary terms of imprisonment. Not only did the cause of English Catholicism seem likely to be lost by default, but the whole future of religion to be decided by relative volume of noise.

To such an eventuality Mary could not well remain indifferent. What directly moved her to intervene, however, was less the threat to religion than concern for the public peace. From controversies which she could only embitter, her sense of her position bade her hold aloof, but the tranquillity of the kingdom was not a matter for controversy; rather were the rights of controversy subordinate in her view to the good order which it was the first duty of government, any government, to maintain. This principle the Protector had, by acting on the opposite view, submitted to an empirical test of which the ensuing disorders were the incontrovertible result—a result to which she felt bound to call his attention in the hope that it might be amended once the cause was made plain. 'The most part of the realm,' she pointed out, 'are now brought into such a division . . . that . . . they will forsake all obedience unless they have their own wills and fantasies, and then it must follow that the King shall not be well served, and that all other realms will have us in obloquy and derision, and not without cause.' By way of illustration she invited him to compare the state of affairs at present with 'the godly order and quietness' left by the King her father, 'at the time of his death' when 'the spirituality and the temporality of the whole realm did not only, without compulsion, fully assent to his doings and proceedings, especially in matters of religion, but also in all kinds of talk,' as she herself offered to bear witness. The remedy was simple and obvious. Henry's successors must take steps to bring the doctrinaires and the windbags, the malcontents and the crackpots, back 'to that stay' in which he had left them.

A quietness predicated upon the Six Articles, 'the whip of six strings,' a 'stay' procured with the aid of the cell, the rope and the axe, will not commend themselves to many in our time or in our particular part of the planet. But it is important not to confuse dislike for uniformity of belief as an end with disgust at the means employed to achieve it, else the dominating problem of the sixteenth century will be incomprehensible. For a thousand years uniformity of belief had been the rule, often challenged but never disproved by schismatic exceptions. Upon it had rested a European society the vast majority of whose members could even yet not imagine any other basis upon which men could live peaceably together. The Reformation had broken the uniformity but without any thought of questioning the rule: on the contrary, its doctrine of *cuius regio eius religio* explicitly affirmed the subjection of belief to the compulsion of power, and one of the few common aims of its many artificers was to extend its sway to the farthest boundaries of Christendom. The idea of toleration simply did not enter in, merely that of survival and ultimate domination. Toleration is a great good, but unless it already resides in the minds and wills of those who are to practise it, it is meaningless. To us the idea of freedom of worship comes easily because religion with its consequences for eternal salvation is no longer a burning issue, because within the walls of our secular institutions we no longer feel ourselves to be so thinly separated from social and political anarchy, because, in short, a uniform system of worship has ceased to be indispensable to an organised system of society. To measure the wisdom and virtue of another age by our possibilities instead of its necessities is to treat history too much in the spirit of the traveller in whom unfamiliar places and persons beget an increase of self-satisfaction rather than of understanding.

That is, of course, but one aspect of the matter. Men may allow for other men's motives and still be appalled by the horrors to which they gave rise. If, as some philosophies hold, man himself is a mere accident of history, these can evidently be dismissed as no more than natural consequences, as most regrettable by-products, of the given historical situation. Necessity knows no law, the end justifies the means. But if man is a moral being owing responsibility beyond the transient facts of history, his acts and his attitude towards them take on another significance. The law *is*, whether necessity knows it or not, and under it who wills the end wills the means. One may not set one's heart upon a good, whether it be unity of belief or a swift victory in war, and disclaim all part in the expedients by which the good has been procured. Yet it is helpful to remember that this hard truth is not a stone that people of one age may freely throw at those of another. Willing our own ends, we tend to reconcile ourselves to the subsequent means however deplorable; not willing other peoples', we easily recognise that their good was not good enough to extenuate the evil of which they had been guilty in pursuing it. But for them as for us only the ends were foreseen, the means scarcely foreseeable. Even Henry did not cold-bloodedly plan the brutalities his course entailed but had resort to them as the difficulties in his way multiplied. So would Mary's fires presently consume some scores of her subjects in the process of testing her belief that a little timely rigour would put a quick and merciful end to the deadly plague of disunity.

The ground of this belief may perhaps already be discerned in her letter to the Protector. Let him show, it says in effect, that he means to stand no nonsense and there will be less likelihood of any nonsense to stand for, since Henry had already shown those disposed that way what they had to expect; in other words, emulate Henry's firmness of attitude as the surest way of avoiding the need of recourse to his severities. Her reasoning may have been wrong, her sensitiveness to suffering unduly subordinated to considerations of state, but of gratuitous cruelty, the cruelty of fear and spite, her record shows little trace—uniquely little for a Tudor. Indeed her impulses ran all the other way, as her well-wishers noted with alarm when she had the enemies who would have destroyed her at her mercy and granted it freely. Whether her father's 'godly order' reconciled her feelings as well as her judgment to his system of terror it is impossible to say, since it is a question to which she had every motive for witholding the answer. But it is permissible to suspect that, however much she conformed her will to Henry's, her heart never consented to the butchery of her beloved Lady Salisbury and the other friends she missed and would miss ever more sorely. Even conformity has its reservations, and of the mind as well as the heart. She had hers, as we know, about certain of the beliefs Henry had required of her, including his right to require them. She conformed, not out of uncritical assent to a list of propositions, but because she deemed obedience to lawful authority more certainly in the general good, and probably more pleasing to God, than insistence upon her own necessarily partial opinions.

Her adversaries would not have put it quite like this. As Protestants they naturally laid more stress on private opinion and less on outward authority. With regard to the practical duty of obedience, however, they in no wise differed from her. In Henry's time they, too, had conformed with reservations. What they now desired was by the exercise of power to give statutory expression to these reservations—so far as they could agree upon them—with the full intention that they should thereafter be unreservedly obeyed. The question whether it was right or wrong to persecute those who refused obedience did not enter in, merely who was to persecute whom for what. The Protector in his reply to Mary made this quite clear. The unhappy state of affairs to which she directed his attention he ignored, her imputations against himself he dismissed with an arch reluctance to believe that they had 'proceeded from the sincere mind of so virtuous and wise a lady, but rather by the setting on . . . of some uncharitable and malicious persons.' Only with regard to her argument from Henry's example did he venture anything in the nature of a rebuttal, which he couched in the form of ironic wonder at her having forgotten 'what labours, travails and pains' her father had undergone before reducing 'some of those stiff-necked Romanists' to the condition she invited him to admire. The similar exertions imposed upon Henry by the more obstinate Reformers he no doubt considered an awkward irrelevance which the debater's privilege of selection entitled him to overlook; but if he objected to Henry's penal laws in principle—apart, that is, from whom they penalised—it is hard to see why he did not speak up when so peremptorily challenged by Mary instead of keeping his criticisms to himself. Consent had not, however, to be inferred alone from silence: action, too, contributed its proof, in the burning of exponents of the less popular heterodoxies, that the present custodians of truth held no original views on how best to safeguard its purity.

Nevertheless the Protector, for all his shifts to avoid serious argument with a lady, did not wholly neglect the opportunity she offered him. Not Protestant Reform but Papist reaction, he managed to convey, had constituted Henry's principal anxiety and placed the largest strain on his energies: not she, therefore, but he best reflected Henry's mind and the policy he would have wished to see pursued. The importance of the claim can hardly be exaggerated. So thoroughly had the founder of the existing religious polity identified it with his will that men could scarcely conceive of looking elsewhere for guidance in whatever related to it. That it was subject to change they knew, since he had put it through many changes, some quite drastic and perplexing, but these only strengthened the instinct to refer its meaning and working to him. Whichever of the contending parties could persuade the nation that in forwarding its own intention it was but carrying out Henry's would therefore possess an enormous advantage. The difficulty lay in establishing any certain conclusion about Henry's from the evidence available. In his later years, under the influence of Catherine Parr and her circle, he had seemed to be moving in a distinctly Protestant direction; on the other hand he had never more loudly professed nor more fervently practised the Catholicism that emerged from his process of nationalisation. His heir he had caused to be educated by eminent Reformers, yet appointed as his next—and quite probable—successor the daughter upon whom all Catholic hopes were centred. As almost his last act he decreed the extinction of the chantries erected as houses of prayer for their founders in Purgatory, in his will he had endowed a bequest for masses to be said in perpetuity for his soul . . . and died leaving both matters to the care of executors, a large proportion of whom had no belief in masses and a number very little if any in souls.

But if the arguments seemed inconclusive, the power to conclude them now lay at hand. Whether Henry had intended this is also obscure: presumably the reservation to Edward of the right to review his ministers' acts when he came of age took into account that the original balance between them might be upset by one faction gaining control. In the event the balance had been manipulated by the very faction which had most to dread from Edward's not living to come of age . . . a reason the more to act as quickly and irreversibly as possible. There were others as well to spur the Protector on. Henry's debts and his debasement of the currency had left the Crown in grave embarrassment for money. But Henry had also demonstrated more than once how religious reform might be used to relieve financial want. This precedent the Protector had not been slow to follow by concluding the business of the chantries, but what remained of the proceeds after the government's members and friends deducted their shares bore little relation to the needs of the exchequer. There still remained, however, the far greater and no less accessible wealth stored in the parish churches . . . 'the precious utensils which adorned the

altars,' the 'costly hangings', the vestments 'of cloth of
gold and silver, or embroidered velvet', and other papistical refuse whose removal would, in the view of the
austerer brethren, equally accommodate God and Caesar
—although the latter was again to be disappointed when
the final inventories were taken by the alert gentlemen
known as forestallers, 'insomuch that many men's·
private parlours were hung with altar cloths, their tables
and beds covered with copes . . . and many carousing
cups of the sacred chalices.'

For the Protector it should be said that this practice
of defrauding the State of what it had despoiled the
Church encountered his sincere disapproval and determined though unsuccessful efforts to stop it. Without a
thorough preliminary cleansing of private morals, which
admittedly stank to heaven, the task was hopeless, while
his impatient supporters were little likely to dally over
honest administration of the public property in preference
to getting on with the job of liturgical reform. There
were, moreover, in both the financial and the theological
connections, his colleagues to consider. Few historians,
regardless of creed, have found a flaw in the title of the
Protector's Council to be the most corrupt, incompetent
and faithless body of men that ever crunched the sweets
of rule in England. The few who were honest were not
strong, the one strong one, John Dudley, Earl of Warwick, was utterly without honesty (unless to have been
fathered by a notorious extortioner was to come by
dishonesty honestly), and the rest were mainly concerned
to extract a price for their weakness most nearly corresponding to their greed.

By contrast with the rest Warwick stood out from the
beginning as an alternative leader, though on behalf of
what principles no one could have said, except insofar
as the zealots answering to the description of 'hot gos-
pellers' hopefully acclaimed him, on the strength of his

fluent command of the idiom of piety, their Moses and
Joshua for the pending journey to the promised land.
Their influence, despite their comparatively small number, was considerable amongst the commercial and
industrial classes, particularly in the City of London,
while their views received vigorous pastoral and parliamentary expression from some of Henry's newer bishops.
Spurred to action by these various incentives, the Protector took in hand a Bill for the establishment of religious
conformity which, much modified in passage, secured the
approval of Parliament at the end of January, 1549.

The Act as it emerged disappointed the Protestants
almost as much as it dismayed the Catholics. Protestant
it undoubtedly was, with Cranmer's Book of Common
Prayer to formulate its system of worship and a punitive
clause to forbid the sacrifice of the Mass. But the mode of
definition was so imprecise as to leave the meaning of
vital articles ambiguous to the present day, while the
methods of enforcement fell short of the ideal at which
according to contemporary standards they should have
aimed. There was no death penalty to eliminate the
irreconcilable, (the heretics mentioned above were
reached by other laws), nor did the fines and imprison-
ments designed to prevent the celebration of the Mass
extend to wilful absence from the prescribed substitute,
so that by the simple expedient of staying away from
church the provisions of the Act could be avoided altogether. Pressed from all sides, the government was too
weak, its members on the whole too spiritually indifferent,
to venture to impose the single iron discipline its more
ardent supporters desired upon a people rapidly dis-
integrating into an aggregate of factions each determined
to have its own way. Having made their law so supple
and its sanctions so mild, the Protector and his colleagues
hoped that their moderation might be imputed to them
by all reasonable folk for righteousness.

The hope was not altogether disappointed. At no time perhaps have the majority of a nation been prepared to suffer serious hardship for their faith and least of all at a time when their minds have been confused as to its essentials. For all the readiness of so many of all creeds to fight and if necessary to die for what they believed, the religious temperature of the age had sunk too low to kindle any similar fervour amongst the generality, for whom the State personified in a visible monarch had come dangerously near to taking the place of an invisible God as their primary object of reverence. In England this mood had been fortified by recent circumstances: after so many changes in so few years, the ordinary individual could hardly help wondering whether one more or less particularly mattered. A visiting observer even went so far as to question whether Englishmen would make any difficulty about professing themselves Mahomedans or Jews if the King told them to. The ordinary individual, his own inner light burning thus feebly, could moreover look to the Church for little guidance in his perplexities. From the parish clergy he had been too long accustomed to receive instruction which reflected only too well the sloth and ignorance which honest Catholics were helpless to defend against the angry derision of honest Protestants; his natural spiritual leaders, the bishops, with few exceptions equally failed him in this crisis, since if he stopped his ears to the vigorous minority who affirmed the new doctrines, he found that the timorous majority had no excessive difficulty in conceding that what they had hitherto taught as error might be received as truth when corroborated by the power of the State. How the few exceptions were dealt with has already been indicated. With the public mind in confusion and leadership in default the next and (as it was hoped) irrevocable stage in the conversion of England from its ancient faith seemed likely to be accomplished with encouraging ease.

Before that consummation could be pronounced, however, one serious obstacle remained to be overcome. It was not a task the government approached with relish. The heiress to the throne could not very well be removed from office nor consigned to prison like a difficult bishop in order to procure her silence. Not only was her person all but sacrosanct, to the perplexed and inarticulate majority it represented their best hope for the future and stay in the present—on this point their current rulers harboured no illusions. Moreover, behind her, ready to interpret any indignity to her as an injury to himself, loomed her cousin the Emperor, with whom they had no wish to be embroiled. On the other hand, to refrain from requiring her conformity to the law, or even tacitly to overlook her breaking it, would afford a demonstration of impotence on the part of the authorities for which the latent forces of resistance were intently waiting. After some hesitation the Council decided to serve formal notice on her that when the new Act came into effect the following Whitsun she would be expected to obey it.

CHAPTER SEVEN

The Greater Defiance

She knew what was coming and to the best of her ability made ready to meet it. This time there was to be no doubt of what to expect on either side, nor any confusion on her own. Not only was the issue greater than it had been thirteen years before, it was also plainer: whatever room there might be for dispute over the Pope's primacy in the Church, there could be none as to the place of the Mass in the Christian scheme. This was the core of the matter, but she had other observations to make and made them in her letter to the Protector rejecting the Council's demand:

'It is no small grief to me to perceive that they whom the King's Majesty my father (whose soul God pardon) made in this world of nothing, in respect of that they be come to now, and at his last end, put in trust to see his will performed, whereunto they were all sworn upon a book (it grieveth me, I say for that the love I bear to them) to see how they break his will, what usurped power they take upon them, in making (as they call it) laws, clean contrary to his proceedings and will, and also against the custom of all Christendom, and in my conscience against the law of God and his Church, which passeth all the rest. But though you among you have forgotten the King my father, yet God's commandment and nature will not suffer me to do so, wherefor with God's help I will remain an obedient child to his laws as he

left them, till such time as the King's Majesty my
brother shall have perfect years of discretion, to order
the power that God had sent him, to be a judge in
these matters himself, and I doubt not, he shall then
accept my so doing better than theirs, who have taken
a piece of his power upon them in his minority.'

Against Henry she had lodged the same appeal to conscience only to withdraw it. One day not far distant the
appeal would be made against her and she would disallow
it. The foregoing letter, whose contents she was to go on
repeating in almost the same words throughout the
struggle before her, reveals how for herself she resolved
this most troublesome of human dilemmas. She did
not dispute the State's right to make laws binding on
its subjects, merely the right of an ephemeral lot of politicians, 'made in this world of nothing', to behave
as if they *were* the State. Even kings might not do this,
at least in England: a hundred years later a king was
beheaded who was accused of trying to. The gist of the
accusation would be that he had broken faith by setting
himself above the immemorial laws of the realm. It was
precisely this charge that Mary now brought against her
brother's ministers: men deriving such authority as they
possessed neither from God nor the consent of the nation
but from the instrument by which Henry had appointed
them for a temporary and limited purpose. Laws of
course needed changing from time to time, but who were
they to undertake changes which went utterly beyond
any present and particular need in order to assail those
deep-rooted, abiding fundamentals in the life of a people
which permanent institutions like states existed to safeguard? To this primary duty the king, as responsible
head of the state, dedicated himself when swearing to
uphold the ancient laws and customs at his anointment—
an act of consecration carrying the same meaning as

Samuel's delivery of kingship to David and analogous to the apostolic transmission of the powers of priesthood. Henry's innovations in the government of the Church might thus be allowed, together with his claim to have left its essential doctrines untouched, because it could be assumed that he had been given the necessary grace to guide him.

The Protector and his colleagues could put forward no such assumption. They were but caretakers 'put in trust' by Henry 'to see his will performed, whereunto they were all sworn upon a book', and to invoke the Holy Spirit to justify their breach of their oath was sheer presumptuous blasphemy. Any novelties they introduced could only emanate from their own wilfulness: as was evident from their breezy supposition that they were capable of answering questions which no state was competent even to entertain. In short, to Mary's mind— and not hers alone—power wrongly used was even more odious, more flagrantly 'usurped', than power wrongly gained, since time might ratify the second—as it had with the Tudors—but nothing could ever set right the first. Where the case was so clear, the good subject's duty to obey was superseded by the free moral being's duty to resist. 'I have offended no law,' as she succinctly explained in a subsequent letter, unconsciously paraphrasing Magna Carta, 'unless it be a late law of your own making, which in my conscience is not worthy of the name of law.'

Yet resolute and at times scornful as was her bearing, she did not conceal from herself that she was frightened. The means of torment available to her enemies were many and subtle, even if they did not dare to offer violence to her person. The same immunity did not extend to her friends and dependents, including the ministers of her faith. Not only could she be made to suffer in and through them, she could also be made to suffer without them, in helpless isolation from the world in which her cause sank to decay and cut off from the sacraments which gave the cause its meaning. From these fears, there was only one person on earth who could conceivably deliver her, the imperial cousin who alone amongst her well-wishers inspired her enemies with awe. But at 33 she was no longer so naive as not to realise that the good will of an Emperor might be subject to other considerations than her need. With anguished yearning she sought and presently made an opportunity to inquire what he was prepared to do. His new ambassador, Francis van der Delft, who had succeeded Chapuys on the latter's retirement because of illness, was invited to present a letter for her from his master at a formal audience. Neither the occasion nor the letter admitted of confidences, the Council being privy to both and two of its representatives present with van der Delft. But after the formalities Mary contrived to have him brought to her privately. She then eagerly demanded whether he had any further word for her. Quickly and quietly he conveyed certain assurances he had received from the Emperor to be delivered to her orally, of his enduring affection for herself and admiration for her conduct, his certainty that she would not falter and his determination to stand by her. Emotion at first rendered her unable to speak, but presently it came pouring out—ejaculations of gratitude, a confession of the fears nothing would induce her to admit to her adversaries, a fervent promise to be worthy of her cousin's trust come what might. From its place of concealment about her person she produced a tattered letter which, she told her visitor as she extended it, she had received from his master twelve years before and carried about with her ever since—quite possibly the very one he had written her in answer to Chapuys' appeal for a message of comfort from him after Henry had finished with her.

Van der Delft, touched, promised to do his best and in fact made himself her untiring advocate with both the Emperor and the Protector. She herself a few days later wrote to Charles restating her case in terms of such desperate appeal that only its forlorn dignity saved it from shrillness. The Emperor responded with an order to van der Delft to go to the Protector and procure a formal exception for her from any law restricting the practice of her religion. Van der Delft went and after a lengthy argument obtained, if not the document he sought, at least a verbal undertaking that if she did not advertise it too publicly 'she shall do as she pleases till the King come of age.' At any rate, so van der Delft reported, and the fact that Somerset later repudiated the promise was less a proof that he had not made it than that, with his fatal proneness to exaggerate his influence over his colleagues, he found himself unable to make it good. For they refused to endorse it, and at a full meeting of the Council decided to send two of their number, the Lord Chancellor Rich and the Secretary, Sir William Petre, to Kenninghall, whither Mary had moved for Whitsun, to instruct her and her household in the new ritual.

They arrived, and the scene with the commission led by Norfolk years before was repeated, but with important variations. Immediately on receiving notice of their coming, Mary had written to van der Delft for guidance. His letter, like the composite echo of so many of Chapuys', stressed the wisdom of not antagonising her visitors: of saying no in so amiable a manner that, though unable to mistake her meaning, they would be practically as pleased as if she had said yes. This feat accomplished, she was not to be alarmed since the Emperor was behind her, and not to hesitate, should she be deprived of her own priests, to avail herself of one of his. From first to last her dependence on her Spanish protectors seemed to disclose the same disconcerting rift between their politics and her principles, they anxious to keep her quiet in their common interest and she not to be found wanting in zeal for what she took to be their common cause.

On the present occasion she followed van der Delft's advice as she had followed so much of Chapuys', namely up to a point. To Rich and Petre's demands, presented immediately on their arrival, she returned a refusal that was quite unmistakable and no more amiable than courtesy required. Not only would she not allow the new ritual to be introduced, she would not even allow it to be explained as the Council had ordered. When the emissaries protested, she flatly rejected their authority over her or hers, and when they intimated that she might be exposing the members of her household to penalties, declared that her servants were her responsibility, which she would not shirk, and declined to discuss the matter further.

Unfortunately for the government's two spokesmen, they could not retort in kind. Instead of proceeding despite her to lay down the law or, better yet, invoking it by summoning the local constabulary to do its duty, they had lamely to produce the second part of their instructions. Sorely pressed by French successes against the English force struggling to maintain a foothold across the Channel, the Council was about to send Sir William Paget to solicit the Emperor's aid. Were he to carry with him a letter from Mary commending him and his errand to her cousin's friendly notice, she would be rendering a distinct service; would she, inquired her visitors, consent to copy such a letter after a form they had brought with them and sign it as from herself? She replied that she would, subject to the stipulation that if they persisted in harassing her she be allowed a postscript informing the Emperor of their conduct in her own words. Judging that the letter would serve its purpose better without, they elected to leave it as it was, and on this understanding Mary received the Sacrament on the feast of the Church's foundation according to her wont without being obliged to borrow a priest who would in any event not have arrived in time.

But if she had won her point, the Council had also gained theirs. Paget could now depart with her endorsement: and though the Emperor had meanwhile reiterated his wishes on her behalf, he still refrained from committing himself to any retribution beyond the pains of his displeasure. These the Council decided to risk and leave the explanations to Paget while they took their next proceedings against Mary. This time, instead of sending to her, they required her to send to them. The order for the reformed service which Rich and Petre should have given was renewed in peremptory terms and, that she might thoroughly understand what was expected of her, a summons dispatched commanding the attendance of the Comptroller of her Household, Sir Robert Rochester, and her chaplain, Dr. John Hopton, to receive the government's injunctions in person for the purpose of imparting them on their return.

It was the move which had all along been in the forefront of her dread. Either these intimate servants and friends would be forced to serve as instruments of interpreting the Council's will to, and be made responsible for imposing it upon, their fellows or, if they refused, be separated from her and exemplarily punished. Though ill again and struggling with a profound depression—twice in five days she alluded to 'the short time I have to live'— she returned a spirited refusal:

'The chief charge of my house resteth upon the travails of my said Comptroller, who hath not been absent from my house three whole days since the setting up of the same . . . so that if it were not for his continual diligence, I think my little portion would

not have stretched so far. My Chaplain by occasion
of sickness hath long been absent and is not yet able
to ride; therefore, like as I cannot forbear my Comptroller, and my priest is not yet able to journey, so
shall I desire you, my lord, and all the rest of the
Council, that having anything to be declared to me,
except matters of religion, ye shall either write your
minds or send some trusty person, with whom I shall
be contented to talk, but assuring you that if any
servant of mine, either man or woman, or chaplain,
should move me to the contrary of my conscience, I
would not give ear to them nor suffer the same to be
used in my house . . .'

Even had they believed her the Lords of the Council
were in no mood to relent, but events had by now given
them an excuse for not believing her. She herself touched
upon it in another letter to the Protector of the same date,
22nd June, in which, after again justifying her refusal to
submit her conscience to his laws, she added the pointed
reminder that 'what fruits grow daily by such change,
since the death of the King my father, to every indifferent
person well appeareth, both to the displeasure of God
and the unquietness of the realm.' Even a person so little
impartial as the Protector would by then have found the
force of her allusion difficult to avoid. The introduction
of the new service on Whitsunday had started a series of
disturbances which, beginning in the West Country,
were soon to spread rapidly to the north and east. Though
apparently disconnected as yet, their spontaneity revealed
a condition of mind capable under proper leadership of
being directed to large-scale rebellion. The obvious place
to look for such direction was the princess whose rank
and popularity uniquely qualified her to voice the hopes
of the dissatisfied, and upon her the government at once
turned its suspicion, believing or affecting to believe

that not only her sympathisers but her active agents were implicated in the outbreaks.

In this they were as wrong in their psychology as in their facts. However good the cause or great the prize, it was no more her style to lead a popular revolt than to emulate her half-sister and barter conformity of creed for immunity from trouble. Trouble she accepted as part of her lot, neither to be embraced nor avoided with thought of profit; the fits of despondency into which she fell when drawn into conflict betrayed how little she shared her father's zest for it as a means to an end or merely for its own sake as a pleasurable stimulant. So remote in the present instance were the present suspicions against her from any foundation in her thoughts that she could hardly credit them with being held seriously. If her accusers cared to look, she wrote back with weary irony, they would find the suspected servants where they belonged, minding their proper business and not off meddling with disaffection which in any event had little need of encouragement from them. Unable to gainsay her but still unconvinced, the Council merely repeated its former summons with the name of one of the most valued of her intimates, Sir Francis Englefield, this time added, together with an imperative reminder of the duty owed to the King and the peril of neglecting it.

This was another matter, not of theology but of treason, the contemporary State's unanswerable because literally crushing retort to disobedience. Mary, knowing herself unable to excuse her three servants from this call upon their allegiance and therefore helpless to shield them from the consequences of disregarding it, allowed them to go after discharging her heart in a letter brimming with bitterness at the inhumanity shown 'to my poor sick priest' and the disrespect shown to herself, 'not doubting but you do consider that none of you all would have been contented to be thus used at your in-

feriors' hands; I mean, to have your officer, or any of
your servants, sent for by force (as ye make it), knowing
no just cause why'. Her normal subscription, 'Your
assured friend to my power', she altered to, 'Your friend,
to my power, though you give me contrary cause.'

The Protector took no notice. There was little purpose
in exchanging recriminations with her when he could
express himself with surer effect through her servants.
Having induced her to send them, he next overrode her
resolution 'not to give ear to them.' A blend of argument
and abuse persuaded Dr. Hopton to carry back a detailed
statement of the Council's wishes, compiled and annotated
with a view to anticipating any further discussion, and to
undertake the task of expounding them to the inmates
of Kenninghall. Mary had no option but to hear him out:
a concession motivated, as she explained to van der
Delft, by the desire to avoid giving the impression of
blind bigotry, but even more, as van der Delft well
understood and told the Emperor, by the fear of what
would happen to Hopton if he returned with his errand
unfulfilled. The government appeared to have cornered
her. Either she must suffer those with whom she lived in
mutual affection and dependence to be set round her as
informers answerable for her misdemeanours or to be
taken from her as delinquents.

At this point events granted her a respite. The disturbances in the West Country and East Anglia had
swiftly grown into formidable insurrections. The French
took advantage of the government's preoccupations
to mount an attack on Boulogne, which the English
had taken some years earlier and held by virtue of a
treaty until a stipulated sum was paid to redeem it. Van
der Delft also saw a chance to turn the occasion to advantage and sought another interview with the Protector.
Recalling the latter's promise to let Mary be, he accused
him of having broken it by his manner of dealing with

her servants and intimated that unless her immunity were
honestly respected, the Emperor would be constrained
to take steps other and more disagreeable than mere
verbal complaints. With the country aflame east and
west, the French threatening to the north, from their
base in Scotland, as well as the south, the Protector could
not very well afford to add the master of Spain and the
Low Countries to the number of his enemies. After some
argument touching Mary's susceptibility to the law and
his doubts of her loyalty, he finally conceded her permission 'to do as she pleases quietly and without scandal'
if she did not wish to conform. But he had given this
undertaking before and the Emperor, on being informed,
instructed his ambassador to return and declare that he
would not be satisfied until the promise had been put
in writing in legally binding form.

What then happened seems impossible to determine
precisely. Apparently the Protector agreed and a letter
was prepared for the King to sign which accorded her
permission to have her own priests and not more than
twenty of her household whose presence she would specifically report by name. According to the same source
Edward, when signing the letter, added the request that
she would seek instruction from 'some godly and learned
men' of her own choosing so as to overcome her 'grudge
of conscience' and thus justify 'the good affection and
brotherly love which we bear towards you.' Certainly
the addition was characteristic of the young King's
feelings throughout. While deploring his sister's attitude,
he retained his affection for her undiminished. Sometimes
with petulance at her obstinacy, sometimes with tears
at the thought of her soul in peril, he endeavoured to
convert her whenever opportunity offered, but despite
his disappointments never ceased to take a particular
delight in the rare occasions on which they could be
together.

Whether or not the dispensation was given in the form demanded, Mary was left comparatively untroubled during the stormy remainder of 1549. The demonstrations against the Prayer-Book in the West were bloodily suppressed, the French halted at the approaches to Boulogne, the East Anglian insurgents advancing under the brothers Kett overwhelmed in battle by the Earl of Warwick with a force of German mercenaries luckily at hand. All in all it had been a close thing and the Protector, whose credit had never entirely recovered from the execution of his brother for treason the year before, now paid the price of failure. Over-optimistic about his power to conciliate and compose, prone to under-estimate the religious and economic tensions of the time, his good intentions had been effectual chiefly in stirring up tumults which he had savagely to quell. With the masses he was still popular, but the ruling classes, stark terrified by what they had escaped, suspected him of meditating further attempts at conciliation when what the situation in their view required was implacable repression. Almost with one accord they turned to Warwick, who had just saved them from the oncoming hordes of maddened peasants, and by October Somerset was in the Tower and Warwick in all but name ruler of England.

On the surface the change appeared to be to Mary's advantage. Warwick had taken his help where he could find it, and in preparing his palace revolution pretty well managed to convey the promise of all things to all men: and while the humbler Protestants dreamed dreams of more perfect reform combined with a fairer distribution of wealth, and the City merchants had visions of a higher synthesis between radicalism in religion and an unbending regard for the rights of property, the Catholics made ready for the reaction which certain solid facts appeared to assure. Not only had Warwick openly courted them and leaned conspicuously on the small Catholic nucleus in the Privy Council; amongst his first acts by which he sought to consolidate his position was an appeal for the good will of the Emperor and the Lady Mary. To each he offered a respectful explanation of what had happened and why, adding for Mary's benefit the news that he had frustrated only just in time a design of the late Protector's to accuse her of treasonably conspiring with him to have herself set up as Regent for her brother.

She did not believe a word of it. In fact she refused to believe anything Warwick said until it had been sifted by the Emperor and tested by events. With a penetration into character she did not always show she recognised him for 'the most unstable man in England' and the real motives of his 'conspiracy against the Protector' to be 'envy and ambition only'. His Catholic accomplices (who would shortly be negotiating the price of their release from prison) were the first but far from the last to appreciate the accuracy of her judgment. Every faith he professed he recanted, every allegiance he contracted he betrayed, every adherent he gained he turned into an enemy except for some adventurers like himself who held their fortunes in bondage to his. Consistent only in the pursuit of his own advantage, adept in no political arts save force and cunning, he contrived to bring a distracted people under his sway for nearly four years without policy, principle and almost without friends, and to bully, rob and very nearly ruin them without serious show of resistance. As a triumph of sheer self-assertion his career is without a parallel in English history, even in the Tudor portion of it where the rise of a family like the Dudleys was a commonplace.

His father, Edmund Dudley, son of a small landed proprietor in Sussex, had found his way into the service of Henry VII at the age of 22, shortly after the completion of his legal studies at Gray's Inn and Henry's conquest of the Crown on Bosworth Field in 1485. His success had been swift and spectacular. The new King's most urgent need was for money and Edmund, whose outstanding gift an even more remarkable lawyer, Francis Bacon, described as that of putting 'hateful business into good language', devised means of getting it for him. In conjunction with a colleague similarly talented, Richard Empson, son of a Towcaster sieve-maker, he revived long-abandoned prosecutions and searched out flaws in ancient title deeds, hauled the defendants before judges and juries previously instructed by the whip-and-carrot method, and with the subsequent fines, or previous compositions, enriched the royal coffers. Thus he amassed a large fortune for his master and no inconsiderable one, together with a vast unpopularity, for himself. Henry VIII at his accession took over the fortune but disengaged himself from the unpopularity by yielding to the public's demand for vengeance. Dudley and Empson were tried as traitors, their gains expropriated and their blood attainted.

For Edmund's son John, then aged 9, it was an unpromising start in life. No type of individual aroused quite the same hatred and contempt as the upstart and extortioner in an age sickened by familiarity with both, while an attainder for treason upon the surviving kin was a stigma scarcely less repulsive than leprosy even after the law had pronounced it cleansed. In John Dudley's case this occurred fairly soon, through the good offices of a patron at court with a daughter whom he betrothed to the youth when the attainder was lifted and his inheritance as far as possible restored. At 22 he was knighted for valour in battle during a campaign in France, by 45 he had been made Lieutenant-General of all the King's forces after a career of almost unbroken success by land and sea. Other rewards and honours were granted him—the office of Lord Admiral, the Garter, the viscounty of Lisle. By his peers and the populace alike he was detested for his avarice and arrogance, but from Henry VIII he continued to attract favour not altogether accounted for by his useful abilities. His swarthy good looks and the ease of his triumphs in the tiltyard attested the swaggering virility which seems to have appealed to nearly every Tudor but Mary; the son who most nearly resembled him, Robert Earl of Leicester, was for years to be the prime favourite and reputed lover of Elizabeth, who in so many ways resembled Henry. Upon Edward the fascination exerted by Warwick—as he by then was—amounted almost literally to a spell. The young King could refuse him nothing; in his name the dictator did as he liked with little other constitutional warrant or status. So certain was he of the boy's submission that he presently took steps to have him prematurely declared of age in the full confidence that he himself would go on ruling like mayor of the palace under the last Merovingians.

Nevertheless a Tudor, even at the age of 12, could not be treated as a *fainéant*. Henry's son had a will of his own and a firm belief in the superiority of his spiritual instruction. Had Warwick taken the conservative line in religion he had given good reason to believe he meant to take, it is doubtful if he could have maintained his influence over the boy's mind for all his skilful pretence of consulting and deferring. As it was, in that respect he gave Edward no reason to complain of him, with the result that at the crisis of his fate he would have no reason to complain of Edward. Under Somerset those subtle enough, or determined enough, could still read Catholic meanings between the entrancing lines of Cranmer's first Book of Common Prayer; those desiring but unable to do so might settle the matter with themselves by staying away from divine services altogether. Under Warwick either alternative became increasingly difficult and finally all but impossible. Where previously the doctrine of the Real Presence had been questioned and assailed, now it was on the highest ecclesiastical authority officially condemned. This was the crux of the matter, the primary distinction between Catholic and Protestant which a series of Acts and decrees sought to impress irrevocably upon the senses and habits as well as the minds of the English people.

For the Catholic the special character of the priesthood resided in the power, transmitted by Christ through His apostles, to invoke Him, truly and physically, under the appearances of bread and wine in the sacrament of the altar. If no such power existed, if Christ was but figuratively present, as the Reformers alleged, obviously there was no particular set of men supernaturally endowed to exercise it, and therefore no need to preserve the sharp distinction between spirituality and laity. Already priests had been accorded permission to marry and laymen to receive communion in both kinds, but in comparison with the measures now taken to blur the distinction these were of secondary importance—measures that, by altering the mode, restricted the meaning of ordination, supplanted the mysterious ritual of sacrifice with a commemoration service by abolishing altars in favour of communion tables, stripped the significance of sacerdotal vestments (after a delay caused by fierce dissensions amongst the Reformers themselves) down to that of optional dress for ceremonial occasions. Presently Cranmer's second Book of Common Prayer, approved in 1552, set forth the liturgical consequences of the new order of worship and his Forty-two Articles its system of doctrine. As before, little was searchingly defined—even then the English were observed to dislike definitions—but the English people had little doubt, and other people none at all, that they were being made over into a Protestant nation. Nor could anyone doubt that this time the law meant what it said, even if what it said was still not free

of ambiguity. For declining to approve one or another
of its proceedings six bishops who had prominently
assisted in the earlier stages of reform were deprived and
imprisoned. Under a second Act of Uniformity, passed
in 1552, laymen who failed to attend the authorised
services on the prescribed days rendered themselves
liable to unpleasant disabilities of excommunication,
and those who attended any other service to terms of
imprisonment ranging from six months for the first
offence to life for the third.

Even more conspicuously than before Mary remained
the sole hope of what might otherwise have well seemed
a hopeless cause. For nearly a year after Warwick's
assumption of power the government let her alone. Then
its preachers began directing public attention once more
to her contempt of the law and her two chaplains found
themselves caught in its toils along with various eminent
prelates and heads of colleges; the following year the
promise made to the Emperor by Somerset was repudiated
and she again summoned to conform. The course of the
ensuing conflict would be tedious to rehearse in detail,
since it largely repeated that with Somerset and reached
much the same conclusion. Warwick had no new weapons
to bring to bear on her—the second Act of Uniformity
was not passed until the issue was virtually settled, and
in any event he would hardly have dared to invoke it;
he was merely tougher and more ruthless than his predecessor. Not only her priests but her three principal
officials were committed to prison and kept there. Her
reverence for the wearer of the Crown, which Henry had
so ably turned to account, as well as her almost maternal
affection for her brother, were often and painfully
exploited by the exhortations, at times petulant, at others
touchingly wistful, which Warwick caused Edward to
address to her. It all availed him nothing except to sharpen
his gnawing fear of what would happen should she ever

be in a position to claim a reckoning. To Edward's pleas and demands, whether by letter or in person, she continued to return the answer

> 'that, although our Lord be praised, your Majesty hath far more knowledge and greater gifts than others of your years, yet it is not possible that your Highness can at these years be a judge in matters of religion. And therefore I take it that the matter in your letter proceedeth from such as do wish these things to take place, which be most agreeable to themselves, by whose doings (your Majesty not offended) I intend not to rule my conscience.'

Offended Edward sometimes was, but their meetings still remained occasions to be eagerly sought, and though in the course of them he might wheedle and expound, he never lessened his demonstrations of honour and love.*

The pressure put upon her through her priests and officials she resisted with the same firmness, the same sturdy air of knowing so exactly what she meant that there was even room for humour to break through now and then. In August, 1551, three members of the Council, especially chosen for their conservative leanings, waited upon her at Copt Hall in Essex with instructions to enjoin the new services on her household and to offer her another chaplain and a different comptroller in place of those under arrest. They had no better luck than the delegation come on a similar errand at Whitsun two years earlier.

> 'As for my priest,' she informed them, according to their report, 'I know what they have to do. The pain

---

* Indeed it is stated by a contemporary that he wanted to intercede to have her left unmolested but thought it did not stand with prudence, as the times went. But the authority, a lady in her service later married to a Spaniard, was not altogether trustworthy, nor would such an offer on Edward's part accord with his character.

of your laws is but imprisonment for a short time
(the second and severer Act of Uniformity was still
to come), and if they will refuse to say Mass for fear
of imprisonment, they may do therein as they like,
but none of your new service shall be said in my
house . . .'

The offer of another comptroller 'a trusty skylfull man'
they had brought with them to replace Rochester she
declined as well—'she would appoint her own officers
and had sufficient years for that purpose'—and with the
threat to make known how 'you of the Council' used her—
'you give me fair words, but your deeds be always ill
towards me', she swept out of the room.

The three went outside to wait for one of the chaplains
not present when the rest of the household was charged.
Presently

'the Lady Mary's Grace sent to us to speak one word
with her at a window. When we were come into the
court, notwithstanding that we offered to come up
to her chamber, she would needs speak out of the
window and prayed us to speak to the Lords of the
Council, that her comptroller might shortly return,
for, said she, sythens his departing I take the account
myself of my expenses, and learn how many loaves
of bread be made of a bushel of wheat, and ye wis my
father and mother never brought me up with baking
and brewing, and to be plain with you I am weary
of my office, and therefor, if my Lords shall send
my officer home, they shall do me pleasure, otherwise,
if they will send him to prison, beshrew him if he go
not to it merrily and with a good will. And I pray
God to send you to do well in your souls, and bodies
too, for some of you have but weak bodies.'

There is a sense of anachronism about the scene, especially the end, with the irate little figure at the window considering the puffy cheeks and spindly shanks below and admonishing their owners to see to their souls in view of the evident infirmity of their bodies: a tang in the language as well as the situation reminiscent of the supreme artist in comedy who began to try out his hand some forty years later.

But if she kept up a bold front, in her heart she all but succumbed to despair. Indeed at one time, when it looked as if they might succeed in cutting her off entirely from the practice of her faith, she very nearly abandoned the struggle and planned to take refuge with the Emperor abroad. A complicated design was worked out by van der Delft to smuggle her from Copt Hall to the Essex coast and aboard a vessel waiting to carry her to Flanders. For a moment an outbreak of trouble in the area seemed to have been providentially ordered so as to cover her flight. But van der Delft died in the course of the preparations and the Emperor, never enthusiastic about the proposal, let it drop because he preferred Mary where she was. If anything happened to Edward it was better that she should be on the spot than have to claim her throne from a distance; and meanwhile he would have the burden of maintaining her in the state which her importance as heiress of England rendered decent and desirable. Instead he intimated to her chief persecutor, in March, 1551, that he was prepared to go to war if the old pledge to respect Mary's scruples was not honoured. Mary herself was at Westminster when this message arrived, as Edward recorded in his *Journal*, together with his plea to her of the day before that 'except I saw some short amendment I could not bear it' and her answer that 'her faith she would not change, nor dissemble her opinion with contrary doings.' The Emperor's threat proved decisive in inducing the Council, after some further protest and mutual bluster, to take her at her word. An undeclared truce left Mary the privilege of hearing Mass in private so long as the fact was not broadcast to the world.*

She had gained her point of conscience, or rather the Emperor had gained it for her. But it was not the point she had been trying to make. What she had all along asserted was that any law pretending to alter religion during the King's minority was no law at all; what the government had conceded was that the law should in her case be overlooked for reasons of policy. The distinction was all-important. For the exception might well be taken to prove the rule, since it was not in logic to enjoy the benefit of exemption from a law while denying it a valid existence. And if this were so, if the right might be imputed to the government of the day to lay down laws for religion, what was to stop it from legislating on other such fundamental matters, the succession to the throne for example?

The question was anything but academic: more and more it obsessed men's minds as the enigma of the future resolved itself into the twin speculations on how long Edward had to live and what Warwick would do when he died. With the present he seemed able to cope, ruthlessly but effectively. In October 1551 he had himself created Duke of Northumberland and his followers signalled out for reward in an unparalleled distribution

---

* There seems to be a perplexing contradiction on this point. The contemporary evidence and modern authorities alike agree that Mary thenceforth heard Mass for the rest of Edward's reign; that her three officials were released, the retention of a priest withheld, cf. for example the *Calender of State Papers Spanish* Vol. IV, p. 360, Pollard, *Political History of England* Vol. VI, p. 55. On the other hand, in the next volume of the Spanish Calendar, pp. 14-15, Mary expressly gets the Emperor in a letter dated 13th March, 1553, to intercede so that she may hear Mass, a privilege denied her these two years past. Whether this letter, the original of which is in Vienna, has been correctly dated, I cannot say. It may not be without significance that during Mary's visit to London a month earlier, the question of religion was not raised (Span. Cal. XI, p. 9)

of dignities and honours. Two months later he got rid of the one rival whom he could still regard as formidable: Somerset, with whom he at one time sought reconciliation through an inter-family marriage, at most times waged bitter and inconclusive warfare for the control of Council and Parliament, and finally closed accounts by man-oeuvring him to the block on a charge of felonious conspiracy. Mutterings and incipient outbreaks he took care of by similar methods that kept the headsman busy and the prisons congested. Parliament, which occasionally dared to resist him, he convoked as little as possible, and for his financial needs resorted to another debasement of the currency, the most serious yet, to borrowing abroad at 14%, to suppressing ancient bishoprics and appro-priating their revenues, to plundering the churches of their remaining valuables.

All this could see him through from day to day, but each day added to the hatred closing in like some danger-ous jungle growth and each day shortened his immunity within the shelter of the Crown. Throughout 1552 Edward, racked by a chronic cough, prostrated in quick succession by measles and smallpox, was plainly expen-ding his last reserves of strength. Northumberland's fertile brain began to toy, according to those closely scrutinising his acts for every meaningful sign, with thoughts of curious expedients: a standing army owing its allegiance directly to him, the erection of a Middle Kingdom between the Trent and the Tweed, a secret understanding with France, the alert and unappeased enemy of so many wars, to lend him aid . . . expedients that hung well together, with Northumberland virtually a sovereign in the North thanks to his title and his appropriation of the ancient bishoprics and the French standing in force along the Scottish frontier.

But if Northumberland meditated such ways out, he put them by. Early in 1553 Edward fell ill of a cold while hunting. Mary paid him a visit—her last—and departed anxious but not gravely alarmed. Soon, however, he began to cough blood and complain of constant fever and pains. By April the doctors intimated to Northumberland that there was little or no hope of his recovery. While the world still vaguely pondered strange reports, he was already putting the finishing touches to a plan which, instead of committing him to an open act of war upon the new wearer of the Crown, would enable him by act of law to substitute another wearer and keep control of the Crown himself.

CHAPTER EIGHT

Lady Jane and Lady Mary

That Northumberland was up to something the world soon
began to suspect, what it was he kept concealed until the
last possible moment. The wise took a hint from the
marriage, on Whit Sunday, 21st May, of his fifth son,
Lord Guildford Dudley, to Lady Jane Grey, eldest
daughter of Henry, Duke of Suffolk, one of his closest
allies, and his wife Frances, daughter of Henry VIII's
younger sister Mary. But in the same week were announced other marriages, including that of Northumberland's second daughter Catherine to the son of the Earl
of Huntingdon, a descendant of the House of York with
a contingent claim to the throne, and of another of Suffolk's daughters to the son of the Earl of Pembroke. The
wider the complex of matrimonial alliances, the less could
any definite inference be drawn from it; it merely proved
that Northumberland was in a hurry to recruit strength
by connecting himself with some of the most powerful
in the land. Many thought that he meant to aim at the
throne himself: that he was having poison administered
to Edward, that he meant to divorce his wife and marry
Elizabeth, or even Mary . . . this last suggestion, besides
being intrinsically nonsensical, lost its credit when the
government's preachers began denouncing her in unison
as a bastard and a tool of scheming foreigners to bring
the realm back under the heel of Rome. Nevertheless
Northumberland continued writing her solicitous letters,
sending her almost daily bulletins on the state of Edward's health, plying her with invitations to comfort

him with a visit to his bedside; while as if to show what
he thought of the preachers, he presented her with a
handsome version of her coat-of-arms displaying an
unflawed ancestry. Mary was sufficiently impressed, and
sufficiently disturbed by her brother's condition, to set
out for London, breaking the journey at Hunsdon, her
house in Hertfordshire, about twenty miles to the north.

In the capital gossip swirled through the air like dust
before a storm and tautened nerves to a degree hardly
equalled in its turbulent history. Distinguished public
figures in long robes and short—bishops, peers, judges,
officials and City aldermen—were observed hastening
preoccupied and uncommunicative towards Greenwich
Palace, where the Court was in residence, and returning
to their carriages and barges more preoccupied and
uncommunicative than before. Mysterious comings and
goings by night turned out to have something to do with
the movement of heavy armament from the arsenals
either to the Tower or to the ships downstream whose
crews were being recalled from leave.* The populace
heard by turn that the King was dead, that he was improving and out of danger; but at the end of the month a
printed prayer for his recovery was posted throughout the
city, as a warning to the people, it was thought, and to
sound their feelings. Their response was to leave their
work and make their way by road and river to Greenwich,
where they demanded to see for themselves how the
King was, with the result that he 'showed himself at a
window . . . so thin and wasted that men said he was
doomed'. The following Sunday 2nd July, they came
again, 'but a gentleman of the Bed-Chamber came out
and told them that the air was too chill.'

An anxiety almost equally intense drove similar crowds

---

* Actually three ships were being prepared at the time for Willoughby
and Chancellor's voyage to China (as they hoped) by way of arctic
Russia, but they had nothing to do with the activities here referred to.

into the streets of France and the Low Countries in quest of every scrap of news and conjecture arriving from London. Even the humblest realised the bearing of the English riddle on his life as the member of a nation and a faith. In Paris and Brussels the two rivals in the interminable contest for the mastery of the West studied the almost daily outpourings of their representatives on the spot and considered what action to take on behalf of their respective interests. Henry II of France dispatched his secretary, Claude de l'Aubespine, nominally to inquire after Edward's health, actually to confer with Northumberland on matters so secret they were not committed to paper nor even confided to the resident ambassador, who was then living under Northumberland's own roof; according to Mary's partisans they comprised the surrender of Ireland or Calais in return for French military support of the Duke's project, whatever it might be. Shortly afterwards the Emperor Charles V, acting somewhat more openly, sent a commission of three to join van der Delft's successor, Jean Scheyfve, in London and assist him to carry out the instructions they bore. These directed them to seek an immediate audience with Edward at which they were to convey their master's good wishes and certain messages regarding current political affairs; to tell Northumberland frankly, even before seeing Edward should he so desire it, the purport of their mission; should they find Edward already dead or no longer able to receive them, to use their own discretion in furthering the two primary objects of preventing the French from getting a footing in England and opposing any effort to deprive Mary of her rights; to avert any suspicion of Imperial interference in English affairs if Mary succeeded by recommending her marriage to some suitable Englishman; and to get in touch with Mary and persuade her to promise to make no changes in government or religion and to pardon all offences that may have been committed by those now in power. In one respect the Emperor was not altogether candid, since he had no intention that Mary should marry an Englishman. But in another he was quite sincere, namely that she should secure her throne first and worry about religion afterwards.

Travelling by way of Calais and Dover the three envoys (only the name of one, Simon Renard, need be remembered) reached London on 6th July. Later in the day, possibly quite late if time be allowed for refreshment at their lodgings after their journey and a conference with Scheyfve to bring their information up to date, Sir John Mason, 'a Gentleman of the King's Bed-Chamber, came with two officers to bid us welcome in the King's name and make courteous offers of entertainment.' The next morning, as they were about to forward their request for an audience, they heard that the King had died the previous evening. But they had heard this before, a number of times, and decided to proceed with their request, meanwhile exploring the reasons for Northumberland's furious activities, which rumour was more and more associating with the marriage of the previous Whitsun. They tried also to get in touch with Mary, but heard that she had suddenly left Hunsdon for Norfolk on the pretext of illness amongst her servants but really because of fears for her safety if she came on to London. Later that same day the Council in answer to their request 'sent to tell us that they will speak to the King about it, fix a time according to his Majesty's condition, and let us know some time to-morrow.' On the morrow, 8th July, came a secretary to say that the King 'was unable to grant us audience, as his indisposition kept him most of the day in bed.' Their suspicions had already hardened into a certainty that he would never rise from it again: but only on the 10th did they discover that Edward was already dead on the evening of their arrival when Mason came to welcome them in his name. They also learned that his successor, Northumberland's daughter-in-law Jane, was to be proclaimed at noon 'this very day in the Tower of London and at Westminster.'

This solution to his difficulties had been suggested to Northumberland by the terms of Henry's will. There, it will be recalled, Mary had been named to succeed Edward if he died without issue, and Elizabeth in like case to succeed Mary. So far nothing had been done contrary to accepted tradition, or, in more modern phrase, strict constitutional practice; the King's daughters had merely been restored to the place originally theirs in the natural order of inheritance.* But thereafter occurred two striking deviations from the norm as the result of two deliberate omissions. Rightful succession pertained only to lawful issue; under a previous Act both sisters had been pronounced illegitimate, a disability which the will and the Act predicated upon it passed over in silence; whence it could be argued that they were the beneficiaries of a mere fiat, persons arbitrarily appointed to succeed to the Crown by one law while barred from it because of an absolute impediment by another. The second omission touched the claimant next after Henry's three children. In the normal course this would have been the Queen of Scotland, Mary Stuart, by virtue of her descent from his elder sister Margaret. But her foreign birth and her residence in France, the historic enemy to whose heir she was moreover betrothed, constituted objections which outweighed the claims of precedence and she was passed over in favour of the descendants of Henry's younger sister Mary.

What Northumberland in effect did was to blend the two Acts to his taste. The one disqualified the last

---

* In actual historical fact a female succession had several times been disputed but constitutional argument had long since been abandoned and was not invoked either by Henry VIII or Northumberland.

direct heirs of the reigning House, the other substituted
for the senior next-of-kin the junior: The Duke observing
that if both were taken at their word the Greys' rever-
sionary interest became an immediate one and decided
to give effect to this foreshortening process by means
of a new legal instrument. There were certain tiresome
complications in that the line of the Greys passed first
through Frances Duchess of Suffolk who for his purposes
was quite superfluous, and that in any event Henry's
will contemplated only her male heirs, of whom there
were none. Frances, however, Northumberland persuaded
to waive her rights, whatever they were, in favour of the
reluctant but obedient 17-year-old bride of his son
Guildford, and the remaining complications he surmounted (as he had surmounted others in the past) by
forging interpolations in unsatisfactory documents.

With Edward, whose consent was of course indispensable, he had little trouble. The invalid, precocious and
cold-blooded in general but sincerely devoted to his
creed and almost hypnotically susceptible to his mentor's
overpowering personality, easily took the point that his
sisters might well be led into impure religious courses,
concurred eagerly in the view that he was the young
Josiah called by God to put down the heathen, and gave
his hearty assent to the proposition that if his father could
fix the succession by will, so could he. The fact that Henry
had the authority of Parliament the Duke presumably
did not stress; that aspect of the matter could be considered when the *fait accompli* had rendered such consideration hardly necessary.

When the details had been worked out and recorded
in a document known as the 'devise', the law officers
of the Crown were called in to approve and formally
incorporate them into Edward's will. Shocked and horri-
fied, they at first refused and were told to think it over
and come back next day. They returned to say that they

had thought it over and that it looked more like treason than ever. Edward raged, Northumberland offered violence and expressed readiness to fight a duel on the subject with anybody present, from the chorus of states-men in the background issued murmurs of 'traitor'. Finally, persuaded in part by Northumberland's threats, in part by his promise of all the protection that the Great Seal, a subsequent Act of Parliament and a royal pardon in advance could afford, 'with sorrowful hearts and weeping eyes' they yielded, all but one. On 21st June the will was witnessed by a hundred dignitaries of the Church, State and City, again only one refusing: although another, presently to become and for forty years to remain the chief pillar of the state, William Cecil, later explained that he had affixed his signature with his fingers mentally crossed.

Meantime Northumberland's preparations to make the devise worth the paper it was written on went briskly forward. The King's ships, refitted and re-manned, took their stations off the East Coast to stop the passage of information or of persons in either direction. Arms and 'a great quantity of provisions' were got together from every possible source, and troops raised by the leading conspirators in 'numbers proportionate to their rank and importance'—500 in the livery of Northumberland, it was said, and 300 in that of Suffolk. To prevent Mary's adherents from doing the same thing the more dangerous of them were summoned to London where they could be dealt with as circumstances required. The Mint was already at Northumberland's disposal, and by means of a quick realisation of such Church property as remained unsold and forced loans from the City merchants he concentrated liquid reserves on a scale adequate to any foreseeable emergency. On Edward's death the guards were doubled at strategic points, the Tower and other fortresses put in readiness, the City gates opened later and shut earlier. When, therefore, Jane was proclaimed her peaceful accession seemed assured at every point. True the proclamation, by then no longer a surprise, was coolly received even in Protestant London, and many of the crowd set up a demonstration in favour of Mary, for which a young vintner's apprentice paid with his ears. But Mary's own sympathisers for the most part regarded her cause as lost, and the Emperor's four representatives advised him that they were trying to get in touch with her to advise her to accept the inevitable and compound with the usurper for her life until some change of fortune offered the chance of a counter-stroke.

It took a day, possibly two, before this message could reach her. By the narrowest of margins she had eluded Northumberland's trap and, reversing direction, was riding hard for safety. Precisely what happened was never made quite clear. On 4th July Northumberland had sent her an urgent request to come to Greenwich. Setting out from Hunsdon, presumably the next day, at Hoddesdon she received a warning of what was afoot and that a patrol of cavalry was already on its way to intercept her. Who carried the warning is unknown; one account says a London goldsmith, but more probably it was an inconspicuous servant of some one sufficiently close to events at Greenwich—at least two later disputed the credit—to have gained possession of the facts in time. Unable, obviously, to challenge Northumberland with her information, since he had as yet committed no overt act, she sent the excuse of her servants' illness—a pretext rendered plausible by the season, which nearly every year brought the dreaded 'plague'—and made for the remotest of her houses at Kenninghall in Norfolk.

After her rode 400 troopers under Northumberland's son, Lord Robert Dudley, before her stretched the rutted, dusty roads of some of the most exposed landscape in England. Her first night she took refuge with a Mr.

John Huddleston of Sawston Hall near Cambridge. The following morning she had barely left the house when a party of her enemies from the town set fire to it in the belief that she was still concealed there; from a neighbouring hill she saw the smoke rising before she pushed on to Bury St. Edmunds, where the inhabitants' welcome gave her another brief respite. But at Norwich she was turned away and on resuming her journey heard that her enemies were closing in so rapidly that she disguised herself as a domestic—so it was later recounted—and rode pillion behind one of Mr. Huddleston's servants. Perhaps because the information is less ample and the outcome was so different, her flight is less celebrated than Charles II's after Worcester and Prince Charlie's after Culloden, but it has its resemblances.

Somewhere on the way—the chronology is necessarily obscure, because events were chiefly reported from London, where little was known of Mary except that she was in head-long flight across country—but before she reached Kenninghall, the courier sent by the Emperor's ambassadors caught up with her. Had she taken the advice he brought the story would have had a very different ending. The picture they painted was one of unrelieved gloom— Northumberland's position impregnable, the people apparently resigned to Queen Jane, the French standing by to counter her last possible though quite improbable hope, an invasion in force from Flanders. Any thought of escape abroad she could now dismiss because of the flotilla riding off Yarmouth. All that remained was to make what terms she could before the victor's searching cavalry bore her off.

Mary deferred her answer till she reached Kenninghall on 10th July, the day of Jane's ceremonial entry into London. She then dispatched her own courier to inform the Emperor's ambassadors that she had rejected their advice, sent them a copy of the proclamation she had just issued announcing her own accession to the throne and requested them to send another messenger 'to receive some information relative to her affairs'. The ambassadors, aghast at her folly, wrote to the Emperor in dismay that the messenger could not be sent since all the roads were guarded and she herself surrounded, and asked to be recalled because they were under such suspicion that they could do no further good. Meantime Mary had also sent an offer of pardon to Northumberland and his accomplices if they would forgo further acts of rebellion and make their immediate submission. This plainly shook them but they of course rejected her offer and, after a somewhat superfluous explanation of why she was 'illegitimate and unheritable to the imperial crown of this realm', made her a counter-offer to leave her in peace if she would 'surcease by any pretence to vex and molest any of our Lady Queen Jane her subjects'. Unattracted by their proposal but alarmed by the proximity of their troops, she again took flight and by a swift move to Framlingham in Suffolk, a stronghold of the Dukes of Norfolk which Henry had appropriated after imprisoning the present duke in the Tower, gained the double advantage of delay and a strategically superior base in less open country.

This time she travelled with a larger train than the six gentlemen and two maids who had accompanied her from Hunsdon. Some of the local gentry, and at least one great territorial magnate, had joined her on the way at the head of their retainers. These, though insufficient to hold out against the hostile strength reported approaching, secured her against surprise and became available for other important services. Carrying her proclamation from Kenninghall far and wide across the shires, dusty men on sweating horses delivered to the people of England the tidings that their Queen, if she was to go down, would go down fighting: 'Wherefore, right trusty and well-beloved, fail ye not!' Nor did they. Hundreds had in fact already spontaneously started on their way, now in answer to her appeal thousands took up bow and pike and hastened to their local assembly points. Lords called up their tenants and tenants recalled their labourers from the fields just ripening for harvest; 'innumerable companies of the common people', journeymen and apprentices, formed up under their captains, the needy for such pay as the individual captain could offer, the rest for none at all; such feats of marching were performed, especially by the more distant, that within a few days a host variously reckoned at somewhere between fourteen and thirty thousand lay encamped in the vicinity of Framlingham. Nor was this all, for the crews of the ships stationed off Yarmouth to prevent her flight sent ashore to offer their allegiance and help, together with the use of some precious artillery.

Meanwhile Lord Robert Dudley, having reached King's Lynn in Norfolk, recognised that further pursuit had become impossible and fell back in the direction of Bury St. Edmunds to await reinforcements from London. There the Lords of the Council, self-immured in the Tower the better to keep an eye on one another, reviewed the disappointing facts and agreed that the time had come to force the decision which fraud had failed to procure. 'The drum is beaten here to raise troops,' wrote the still despondent ambassadorial quartette, 'and they are to have a month's pay in advance.' Northumberland offered the command to the Duke of Suffolk as the colleague most likely to remain faithful because of the family interests involved. But at this point Jane herself intervened and with tearful obstinacy besought Northumberland to go instead. Troubled and bewildered at finding herself where she was, she had nevertheless not lost her sense of reality and had no difficulty in measuring the difference between her fatuous parent and 'the best man of warre in her realm'. The Council supported her, and Northumberland, though more than dubious of their motives in pressing him to go, had no choice but to consent.

Through a gaping, silent crowd—'the people prece to see us, but not one sayeth God spede us'—the famous warrior led his army out of London on a rambling march towards Cambridge which seemed to lack any serious military purpose. Indeed his chief concern was to keep watch on the allies he had left behind rather than to make contact with the enemy in front. Apparently he hoped to recruit his force with the peasantry on his line of march, but they slyly eluded him while his own troops melted away either to resume their neglected occupations or to slip across country in the direction of Framlingham.

As Mary in her flight had stirred such depths of loyalty and love, so he in his advance left a trail of treachery and hate. Some of his colleagues tried to decamp from the Tower and were forcibly brought back; others succeeded in getting into secret touch with Mary's sympathisers either to make their individual arrangements or to act as intermediaries for the rest. Within five days of his departure, on 19th July, they reached general agreement that the whole thing had been a criminal blunder for which he was entirely to blame and sent to tell him so. Jane was hustled out and a proclamation given forth announcing the joyous accession of Mary.

The news reached Northumberland at King's College, Cambridge, whither he had fallen back after reaching Bury unopposed. His troops saluted it by firing their guns, the only occasion given them for doing so; he himself, with a cry of ' "God Save the Queen!" tossed his cap in the air, so laughing that the tears ran down his face with grief.' After a brief detention by order of the Mayor, he prepared to leave next day, but before he was fully dressed the Earl of Arundel, the colleague who had last and most fervently sworn never to desert him, arrived with the Council's order for his arrest. Falling on his knees, he reminded the Earl that he had done nothing but 'by the consent of you all', and begged him 'to be good to him, for the love of God.' Arundel silenced him with a prim, 'My lorde, ye should have sought for mercy sooner', and he meekly allowed himself to be led off to London.

So ended, tamely and even preposterously, what had for ten days threatened to be the most spectacular and sinister political adventure in English history.

CHAPTER NINE

The Fair Beginning

Few doubted, any more than did Mary herself, that the hand of Providence had directed the outcome. Victory so swift and sure against all material calculation of odds permitted no other explanation. 'God so turned the hearts of the people to her and against the Council,' confessed John Knox, the implacable enemy responsible for pre-fixing the Bloody to her name, 'that she overcame them without bloodshed, notwithstanding there was made great expedition against her both by sea and land.' That their hearts had been willing instruments of the divine choice the people attested at her entry into her capital a few days later. 'Great was the triumph here,' wrote one observer. 'For my time I never saw the like, and by report of others the like was never seen . . . Money was thrown out of the windows for joy. The bonfires were without number, and what with the shouting and crying of the people and ringing of the bells, there could no one hear almost what another said, besides banquetting and singing in the streets . . .' The celebrations went on all through the night, 'with bonfires in every street, with good cheer at every bonfire, and everybody having every-body else to dinner and the Te Deum sung in every parish church for the most part until the next day at Nones.'

The reign begun amidst such rejoicing was to end a little over five years later in a universal sigh of relief. The sad irony of the contrast lies in the fact that the expecta-tions which inspired the rejoicing were not disappointed but only too well fulfilled. Disillusioned and bewildered by the upheavals of the two previous reigns, culminating in the corruption and near-anarchy of the more recent, the impoverishment of many for the enrichment of a few, the nation turned to its new Queen as the symbol of a by now almost idyllic past. If not fervent about the old religion—though many in fact still were—it was prepared to accept almost any religion backed by sufficient authority to put down contentions and disorders. If not well informed about the system of foreign relations by which her grandfather, Henry VII, had sought, and managed, to avoid foreign wars, the English people understood well enough the contribution of Henry VIII's wars to their various and collective miseries. They knew also that Mary's mother, whom they held in reverent memory, had been the bond and token of the earlier system erected with Spain as successor to the old Burgundian alliance for the containment of France. Then there was the person of Mary herself, the gallant survivor of so many adversities, the long unseen focus of so much hope and affection now at last seen by the cheering multitudes to have been worthy of them: 'The Queen's demeanour,' reported one, 'her gracious modesty, more divine than human, did but enhance them.' The admitted handicap of her sex would be overcome by a suitable marriage and the production of an heir to continue the task of happily reknitting the past with the present and future. What was anticipated of her she attempted, consistently and courageously, yet it all went disastrously wrong. The past proved irrecoverable. She had become an anachronism.

There was perhaps a foreshadowing of this truth when she took up her temporary residence in the Tower, as prescribed by custom, before proceeding to Westminster for her coronation. On the patch of green not very long since stained by the blood of husband, son or parent,

EDWARD VI
by Scrott

ELIZABETH I

*Artist unknown; perhaps from the circle
of William Scrots/Scrott*

inmates imprisoned during the two previous reigns waited to greet her—ghosts from the past for whom, with one exception, the future was to hold less than that joyous moment seemed to promise. Amongst them were her old Gossip (co-godmother to the same infant) Nan, Somerset's widow, the Duke of Norfolk, her premier peer whom Henry's death had saved by a bare few hours from the fate of his gifted son the Earl of Surrey; young Edward Courtenay, heir to the shattered house of Devon and the claims of the White Rose of York to the throne—the favourite of many as prospective King-consort; together with Stephen Gardiner and four other bishops who had been given time to meditate upon the less pleasing aspects of a Royal Supremacy which they had served so usefully only to be served by it so harshly. Mary embraced them one by one, mingling her tears with theirs, and after happily reminding them, 'Ye are all my prisoners,' ordered them released forthwith.

The joys of welcome and reunion were soon over. The new Queen had to grapple with the old truth that not the same modes of thought and action were applicable to government as to opposition. Principle, however fortified by courage, consistency and good will, had to be reviewed in the light of practical possibility. A first example arose almost immediately in the question of her predecessor's funeral. Should Edward's body, which still awaited interment, be buried according to the Catholic or Protestant rite? The Emperor's ambassadors, instructed by their master, urged Mary not to make an issue of the matter; to override the established forms, as well as the late King's own preference as declared in his will, would be certain to start an agitation which it was her first interest to avoid. This view Mary strongly resisted. To refuse her brother the intercessory offices of the Church amounted in her eyes to refusing him, because of a faulty upbringing, a properly Christian burial. The ambassadors, still echoing their master, suggested that for one who had died outside the communion of the Church salvation was already forfeited, her intercession hence to no purpose. This callous (and in fact perverted) dictum Mary let pass unanswered, but to the political argument she was in the end constrained to submit: Edward received a Protestant funeral at Westminster while in the Tower his sister had a Mass said in private for the repose of his soul.

Already it was plain that Mary as Queen would retain as her principal adviser the imperial cousin on whom she had depended for guidance in her tribulations as disinherited Princess. It was a sinister portent. Apart from the resentment with which any proud people was certain to regard the intrusion of a foreigner into its affairs, it was but too apparent that in the nature of the case England could not be other than a single and subordinate factor in any considerations affecting the safety and expansion of the Habsburg empire. Not the least appealing of Henry VIII's reasons for his repudiation of any alien claim to the loyalty of his subjects, whether religious or secular, was that England herself was an autonomous 'empire'. Charles, to whom long experience had brought wisdom, was well aware of these feelings; it was why he instructed his ambassadors, when she proposed to hurry on with the restoration of the old religion,

'to say to her that, as God has been pleased to dispose all things in so excellent a manner, we advise her to take very great care at the outset not to be led by her zeal to be too hasty in reforming that may not seem to be proceeding in a right manner but to show herself to be accommodating . . . Let her dissemble for the present, not to seek to order matters in a manner different from that now observed in England . . . but wait until she is able to summon Parliament . . . in

order to take such measures with its participation . . .
Let her be in all things what she ought to be, a good
Englishwoman . . .'

His concern arose, of course, not out of love for the
English, any more than did his caution a little later to
damp down her religious persecutions issue from any
love of heretics. It was simply that the more of the nation's
good will she commanded the greater would be her use
as an ally—or, more exactly, what we should now call
a satellite.

To Mary the advice was, to say the least, disconcerting.
Dissimulation and delay were the last things she would
have supposed God to have expected of her in return for
disposing things so excellently in her favour. Nevertheless
she could not but allow the force of the Emperor's
admonition. Prudence was, after all, a primary moral
virtue, while to proceed without Parliament in so important a matter would plainly be inconsistent with her
constitutional duty; and for the constitution, in the sense
of fundamental law embodying natural justice and tested
tradition, her respect was as profound as was her contempt for the notion that the value of any given law
resided in the mere power to declare and enforce it. The
ways in which she showed that respect were, in fact,
largely responsible for her early popularity: her severest
critics admit the unusual, virtually unique, fairness of her
Parliamentary elections and the ringing sincerity of her
charge to the Lord Chief Justice of the Common Pleas,
'Ye are to sit here not as advocates for me but as indifferent judges between me and my people.' But if there were
sound reasons for delay she could find none for dissimulation, and from Richmond two days after Edward's
funeral issued a proclamation stating that:

'. . . her Majesty, being now in possession of her
imperial crown and estate pertaining to it, cannot

forsake that faith which the whole world knows her to
have followed and practised since her birth; she desires
rather, by God's grace, to preserve it until the day of
her death; and she desires greatly that her subjects
may come to embrace the same faith quietly and with
charity, whereby she shall receive great happiness.
She makes known to her beloved subjects that out of
her goodness and clemency she does not desire to
compel any one to do so for the present, or until by
common consent a new determination may be come to;
but she forbids all and sundry of her loving subjects,
of every age and condition, under penalty of the
laws to stir up tumult or sedition among her people,
on the pretext of upholding certain laws of the kingdom made according to the fantasies of men . . .'

Her subjects were exhorted not to insult one another by
'words of recent introduction' like 'papist' or 'heretic',
unauthorised persons were forbidden to preach or give
religious instructions, mayors, sheriffs and other officials
enjoined to punish impartially any who committed or
incited to breach of the peace. It cannot be denied that
she was doing the very thing she had reproached the
Protector for doing, permitting and even encouraging
a system of worship which the law forbade. It is difficult
to see what else she could have done short of compelling
her people to do what she herself would have died rather
than do. Having rejected the alternative of changing
the law by arbitrary act, she had no option but to evade it
by proclaiming religious toleration.

Scarcely less novel and hazardous was the solution she
adopted for the other major problem urgently confronting
her. All precedent decreed that the participants in the
late rebellion should receive such justice as would effec-
tually eliminate them and deter others from similar
enterprises in the future. But though alive to the dangers

of neglecting this classic prescription, the Emperor
felt that at the threshold of her reign it might be better
for his cousin to kill as few enemies in the hope of gaining
as many friends as possible: a judgment in which Mary,
as little resentful of injury to herself as she was sensitive
to whatever touched her faith, spontaneously concurred.
Rarely if ever was treason so widespread and flagrant so
leniently punished. Of the scores who conspired and the
hundreds who bore arms against her, no more than a
dozen ever stood in any real jeopardy. Out of a first
tentative list of twenty-seven, only seven were actually
put on trial; Lady Jane, her husband, his brothers Robert
and Henry and Bishop Ridley remained in the Tower for
further consideration; the rest, including Jane's egregious
father, suffered at the worst a few days' detention. The
seven, consisting of Northumberland, his brother Sir
Andrew, his eldest son the Earl of Warwick, the Marquess of Northampton, Sir Thomas Palmer and the
brothers Sir John and Sir Henry Gates, appeared for
judgment at Westminster Hall on 18th and 19th August.
To the acts of which they were accused they had already
confessed, but before the court vigorously argued that
those acts, having the warrant of the Great Seal, were not
legally crimes, and that even if they were, the court was
incompetent to try them because various of its members
were equally implicated. Both pleas were rejected, a
precedent of Northumberland's being cited in over-
ruling the second, and the defendants sentenced to death,
but for all except the Duke, Palmer and John Gates the
penalty was remitted. Even Northumberland expected up
to the last minute to be let off as well; he begged, grovel-
led, offered to—and did—make public profession of the
Queen's faith. But there were limits, and on 23rd August
his head and those of his two confederates fell on Tower
Hill in the presence of an awe-stricken multitude.

Apart from those executed few suffered the other

forms of punishment whereby the Crown on such occasions enriched itself and rewarded its friends. Mary chose to profit otherwise from her clemency. The incriminated law officers she confirmed in their places and of the late Privy Council selected twelve, more than a third, to impart useful strength to her own. Its earliest members she had naturally selected from her immediate circle, men like Rochester, Englefield and Waldegrave who had stood by her to their own hurt under Edward and during the perilous ten days of the usurpation. To them she added as opportunity offered various of her father's former ministers who had refused to come to terms with Somerset or Northumberland, notably the Duke of Norfolk, some lesser peers and the deprived bishops of whom the foremost, Stephen Gardiner, became her Chancellor. Those of the first group, appointed primarily for their loyalty, had little experience or public influence; those of the second possessed the experience but had been associated with Henry's persecution of Mary and her mother, and though they had undergone a change of heart for which they had paid with loss of place and in most cases of liberty, that in itself had long kept them out of touch with public affairs. Hence mere good sense prompted Mary to retain in her service members of the previous Council like Paget, Sir William Petre with his ten years of service as Secretary of State and William Paulet, Marquess of Winchester, whose administration of the Treasury reached back into the time of Henry and would reach well forward into the time of Elizabeth: content to be 'a willow rather than an oak' and change his religion as often as necessary to keep his job. A policy of reconciliation also necessitated the retention of great territorial magnates like the Earls of Bedford, Pembroke, Shrewsbury and Westmorland with their paramount influence in the West, Wales and the North, while obligations had been incurred during the uprising to several such as the Earl of Arundel, a useful turncoat at a critical moment.

Royal Councils had little in common with the Cabinet system which in course of time evolved from them. They shared no collective responsibility, being answerable only to the sovereign at whose pleasure they held office. They represented no coherent agreement on policy, large or small, but a balance of factional interests and attitudes amongst which the sovereign could choose; if one or other of these came into conflict with a course on which the sovereign had determined, those who differed risked dismissal or even severer penalties according to the gravity of the conflict and the mood of the sovereign, or at the least exclusion from the higher posts through which the main business of government was carried on. Mary's Council was even more varied in complexion than most, for the reasons indicated above. That it survived the revolution, or more precisely the counter-revolution, for which Mary recruited them is a remarkable commentary on Tudor polity and those who served it. Equally remarkable is the fact that while co-operating in activities with which many disagreed and which all could presently see were hurrying the country to disaster, they carried through administrative reforms which laid the foundation for the triumphant recovery under her successor.

Only in this century has the administrative as distinct from the political aspect of Mary's reign been objectively examined. Until then it was assumed that the one shared the ineptitude and failure of the other. Now even her severest critics are prepared to modify the view which formerly her warmest defenders did not seriously question. A detailed survey of the scholars' labours, pertaining as they do to the field of social history, would be out of place in a mere biographical study. Their concern is with the collection and analysis of figures, of sums of money collected and distributed, the mechanism and assessment of the royal financial structure. But the conclusions are relevant and clear. The extortions, corruption and waste of the two previous reigns were sharply checked. The pillage of religious, the impositions on private property (devised largely to balance the deficits caused by a series of senseless wars), the diversion of a great part of the proceeds into the hands of the favoured and powerful— these practices not only ceased but something was restored to the Church and private individuals relieved by a much-appreciated remission of a subsidy reluctantly granted by the previous Parliament. The many bodies entrusted with the gathering and spending of the revenues were called to a strict accounting; their efficiency, honesty, even their necessity were looked into and various of them, including the notorious Court of Augmentations created by Henry to deal with the spoils of the Church, dissolved. The crown lands were no longer sold and their revenues steadily increased, the customs schedules were reconsidered and revised with a substantial increase in their yield, pensions and annuities that could not justify themselves reduced or terminated. The final judgment of a leading authority on Tudor finances holds that 'Mary's government was strong and capable enough to gather together the remaining resources of the old system, and so conserve, husband and increase their productivity, that, with the careful parsimony of Elizabeth it worked for another half century.' If Mary did not contrive these reforms, they could not have been carried out without her encouragement and approval, and certain of them at least would not have been initiated without 'her sense of stern honour and exact justice.'*

* For the foregoing I have relied chiefly on C. Dietz's study of the *Finances of Edward VI and Mary*, Vol. III, No. 2 of Smith College Studies in History, January 1918. It should be added in fairness that certain of the reforms had been under consideration before Edward VI died, but nothing was done about them.

CHAPTER TEN

The Sorrowful Ending

The events of the reign are too well known to bear extensive retelling. Its reputation, and Mary's, have long been established and seem unlikely to be much modified. The chances are remote that new evidence will be discovered, a more favourable judgment passed on the persecution of heretics or the marriage with Philip of Spain which constitute the two chief grounds on which the condemnation alike of contemporaries and posterity have rested. The testimony of the *Book of Martyrs* will doubtless continue to be scanned and weighed, instances of prejudice or ignorance adduced, individual victims removed from Foxe's list of sufferers and others previously removed restored to it; but the number is likely to remain near his total of something under three hundred, their concentration within a restricted area and social class undisputed, the effect of horror he intended and achieved undiminished.

The marriage with Philip falls into a different category of culpability. The persecutions could not have been carried on without her consent and would hardly have been undertaken without her encouragement. But if she may be held ultimately responsible, she was not directly or exclusively so. However enthusiastically her officials might receive the delations of suspected heretics, the investigation, trial and sentence were matters for the bishops' courts, whose order as to punishment admitted of no appeal or evasion by the secular authority. Many have tried to allocate precise responsibility for the holo-

caust, none has ever succeeded in satisfactorily doing so.
No such ambiguities surround Mary's choice of Philip
to be her husband. It was her own entirely, made against
the objections of nearly all her advisers and in defiance
of a dangerous popular opposition. It was intended,
and opposed or upheld, as a political transaction. As such
it turned out to be a disastrous error. But it turned out,
unexpectedly, to be something else as well, a catastrophe
for her as a woman which would reveal as yet unsuspected
depths in her character and compound political error
with hopeless personal misery.

Her marriage was amongst the first questions discussed with the Spanish emissaries at New Hall before
her entry into London. That she would marry was
taken for granted, if only to ensure the succession, but
potential bridegrooms were not yet openly discussed.
Yet it is impossible to believe, despite the manoeuvrings
of the next few months during which the French did
what they could to divert her thoughts in some other
direction, that she had not from the first set her mind on
Philip. Her whole history inclined her to closer ties with
the Power that had long been her sole support, to the
renewal of the old alliance to which she owed her very
existence; and her eager endeavours to learn all she
could about Philip's person and qualities pointed in the
same direction. The Emperor's wishes of course coincided with hers, but he advised caution until her possession of the throne was sufficiently secure for her to be
able to depend on carrying the country with her. She
on her side had to contend with and in one way or another overcome the opposition of her principal ministers.
Very few apart from Paget, who negotiated the prelimin-
aries, favoured it, and he for reasons that only partly
coincided with hers. The rest, indeed the whole nation,
so far as its opinion could be ascertained, disapproved in
vehement terms. Men of many diverse opinions, with

Gardiner at their head, united in commending to her an alternative in Edward Courtenay, Earl of Devon, whom she had likewise freed from a long captivity in the Tower and who, in his capacity of heir to the White Rose of York would, they urged, gain her considerable support in the country and an unassailable title to transmit to her offspring.

This advice she rejected, as she rejected the advice of various of her friends who would have preferred another descendant of the House of York, her kinsman Reginald Pole, to either Philip or Courtenay. With regard to Courtenay she could object that he had hitherto shown no aptitude for anything but debauchery, but the same objection hardly applied to Pole, a Cardinal of austere life and distinguished learning. For many years he had lived in exile, an attainted traitor because he had championed Catherine and Mary's cause in a notable indictment of Henry; upon his mother, the Countess of Salisbury, Mary's governess and most devoted of friends throughout her unhappy youth, Henry had wreaked the most savage of vengeances, and towards him in consequence Mary cherished feelings of almost boundless gratitude and reverence. But Pole was not the marrying sort for one thing. He was already 54, a priest by vocation though not yet by actual ordination, a scholar by temperament and a recluse by choice. In any event another kind of future clearly awaited him. A few years earlier he might have been Pope had he so chosen and it seemed probable that he would one day again be called and irresistibly. Meantime he awaited the summons from his native land informing him that the time was ripe for him to return and enter upon his mission of reuniting it with Rome. In every other way in sympathy with Mary, who longed to have him with her as ardently as he longed to go, he flatly disagreed with her about her marriage: a prime reason why the Emperor continued to detain him on the continent until the marriage had been accomplished. Not only did Pole not wish to marry Mary himself, he strongly advised her not to marry at all but to devote herself single-mindedly to the task for which Heaven, against all earthly calculation, had so miraculously preserved her. It was the course which Elizabeth was to adopt with such success, though its success might have been less pronounced had not Mary's adoption of the opposite course served as a dreadful warning first.

She affirmed solemnly that she had no other motive in marrying Philip than the good of England and of the Catholic faith, no thought whatever of merely personal or carnal gratification. But though offering this explanation to her kingdom, she furiously declared to its representatives, in the form of a Parliamentary committee come to wait upon her with a remonstrance, that her marriage was no affair of theirs or of anyone except herself. It was the language Elizabeth would use in similar situations, but Elizabeth, with no intention of doing what she was threatening to do, was being disingenuous, 'putting on an act', for her own hidden purposes, while few have ever doubted Mary's honesty or earnestness. Nevertheless, without probing deeper than historical or human decency permit, the facts do seem to suggest that she too had her hidden purposes, hidden at least in part even from herself. She may well have thought she was being sincere in denying any purely personal hankering for a man she had never seen, whom she knew only by description and by a portrait of him they had sent her—possibly the very portrait she would presently fall upon in an anguish of jealousy and tear to strips with her nails. But the denial itself is of such surprising strength, more like a response to a challenge from within than to one from without—which nobody had in fact ventured to offer—that one cannot help wondering what prompted her to make it. Irresistibly there comes to mind a passage from the wonderful letter written to her by her mother in the depths of their common agony ... 'But one thing I especially desire you, for the love you owe unto God, and unto me, to keep your heart with a chaste mind, and your body from all ill and wanton company, not thinking nor desiring any husband, for Christ's passion—till this troublesome time be past.' Did Catherine, knowing and loving her daughter better than any other human being ever had or ever would, suspect the existence of hidden fires that needed to be watched in the frail little body? And was it perhaps Catherine as well as herself that Mary was trying to reassure with her vehemence?

The excessive insistence on principle rather than passion as the motive of her marriage would help to explain her unwonted obstinacy, for though normally humble, even submissive, when proffered advice by others, in matters of what she took to be principle she tended always to be obstinate, as her father and brother and their ministers had been shocked to discover. Of course she expected to love Philip, in accordance with the Christian teaching that love is an act of the will, that the only real love, in fact, is that which has been perfected by the will. So thousands of women had loved husbands whom duty untinged by inclination had chosen for them; so had her mother loved her father despite everything he did to kill her love. But those others, including her mother, had rarely been given her freedom of choice, had from the first fixed upon the husband recommended by duty as the only man in the world they could conceivably marry. They had not betrayed themselves to outsiders by incessant and feverish inquiries regarding his looks, habits, tastes and morals, nor by an only too visible alarm lest he, a widower of 27 with some experience of women, should find her, a virgin of 38, mentally uncongenial and physically distasteful. Not only was she prepared, on the basis of what she could learn, to love but to be hurt by him—quite another story.

Her people were as little disposed for the one as for the other. They disliked foreigners in general, Spaniards on the whole less than Frenchmen though not sufficiently less to feel called upon to aid the former in their interminable war with the latter, as they strongly suspected the Emperor meant them to do in promoting the marriage of his son to their Queen. The marriage contract expressly exempted them in the clearest terms from any such liability, but they did not trust the contract, rightly as it turned out. When the Emperor's envoys came to sign it in January 1554 they were met as they passed through the City by hostile looks and words from the adult inhabitants and volleys of snowballs from the juvenile. Meanwhile, in various parts of the country the chronically discontented, conspicuous amongst them the followers of Northumberland whom Mary had spared the previous summer, were organising those who hated and feared the marriage for armed resistance. The most formidable of these movements, whose object was to set Elizabeth and Courtenay as a wedded pair in Mary's place, had its centre in Kent, perilously close and the more perilous because its leader, Sir Thomas Wyatt, had enlisted the support of France, whose rulers were naturally anxious to prevent any closer connection between England and Spain. The original intention was to wait until the different forces could go into action simultaneously under a pre-arranged plan, but when the government revealed by a number of arrests that its suspicions were aroused, Wyatt was driven to anticipate the plan.

A direct thrust from the Southwark bank of the Thames nearly carried him straight into London, but finding the bridge too well defended he turned west until he reached the crossing of the river at Brentford. From there his advance on the capital not only encountered no resistance but gained strength as it went on. The musters hurriedly summoned by the Queen's military leaders either failed to respond or went over piecemeal to the enemy: most sinister portent of all were the desertions from the City of London train-bands, the best disciplined troops within long reach, for they seemed to confirm the general belief that Wyatt had but to enter the City, where he could count on the overwhelming support of the populace, for his whole venture to be crowned with success. As he cleared the muddy wastes of Knightsbridge the members of the Court began to abandon Whitehall in panic. The Queen's ministers pleaded with her to flee and at least save her person until measures to retrieve the situation could be organised elsewhere. Instead she rode to the City through all the fearful confusion, to a great meeting convoked at the Guildhall, and there, face to face with the men preparing to receive her enemy, spoke her mind in that specifically Tudor manner which somehow never failed to overpower the imagination of subjects faltering in their allegiance: 'What I am ye right well know—I am your Queen . . . like true men stand fast against these rebels, both your enemies and ours: and fear them not, for I assure you I fear them nothing at all.' Hardly was she back in Whitehall than the sound of firing and the clash of arms announced the course of Wyatt's successful thrust past her few defenders towards the Fleet ditch and Lud Gate. There the effect of her recent appeal received its test—a test not merely literary like Elizabeth's great Tilbury speech, which was perhaps never spoken or, if it was, not until the emergency to which it referred had passed. Wyatt found the Londoners waiting not to greet him but to overwhelm him. After a vain effort to push his way through the turgid throng, he sat wearily on a bench before a tavern and watched his followers being disarmed and led away.

Their severed heads soon gave warning from London Bridge and other public centres that Mary did not intend to repeat her previous mistake. Not only Wyatt's chief accomplices but his followers and dupes contributed to the ghastly spectacle; even some who had had nothing to do with him, like Lady Jane Grey and her husband, now paid the penalty for their part in the first rising because of close kin who had abused the Queen's clemency by taking part in the second. Whatever it cost, Mary was resolved that her fiancé should be involved in no unpleasantness at his coming. Even her half-sister and presumptive heir, Elizabeth, came near to being caught up in the holocaust. At the time that the government's suspicions were beginning to be fixed upon Wyatt, Mary had sent her an invitation to come to court where it would be easier to keep a safe distance between her and trouble. Elizabeth answered respectfully, declining on account of the state of her health, into which she entered in some detail. Shortly afterwards the government, by then convinced of Wyatt's treasonable relations with France, had the French ambassador's courier waylaid on the way to Dover and the contents of his pouch stolen for examination. Amongst them was found an exact copy of Elizabeth's letter to Mary: a coincidence of such sinister import that Mary dispatched several of her councillors and physicians with an armed escort to determine whether she could safely be moved and, if it was found that she could, to bring her to Court; whence, after a delay occasioned by her efforts to play upon Mary's feelings, she was shortly transferred by river to the Tower.

The evidence, though ample to warrant her arrest, proved insufficient, however, to justify her conviction. For nearly two months the law officers of the Crown laboured while she, terrified but resourceful, eluded their every effort to establish a criminal understanding between her and Wyatt. He himself, after prolonged

MARY I
by Antonio Moro

PHILIP AND MARY

A medal struck on the Continent
for their marriage

questioning, at length publicly exculpated her from the scaffold.

Mary's dilemma could hardly have been more unhappy. There is little doubt that she had loved Elizabeth since the time that both of them had become motherless orphans of little further apparent importance to the State. 'My sister Elizabeth,' reported Mary to their father in the course of a holiday when the younger child was about 4, 'is in good health, and, thanks be to our Lord, such a child toward as I doubt not your Highness shall have cause to rejoice of in time coming'; there were many holidays spent together, sometimes with Edward also present, many gifts painstakingly worked by each sister for the other on the occasion of birthdays and festivals. It could not have been easy to order the girl's arrest, even after Mary had become convinced that she was a hypocrite in religion and a plotter against her Crown; moreover she would not have forgotten the odium that had fallen on the Protector for prosecuting his own brother, the Lord Admiral Seymour, Elizabeth's late suitor, on a charge of treason even more manifest. Having taken the step, Mary now found herself, owing to defects in the evidence—or, as she bitterly surmised, the zeal of some of her servants—transposed in her people's eyes into the wanton and malicious enemy of Elizabeth the injured victim. There was nothing she could do: her father and grandfather would have found ways, but for Mary, with her scrupulous respect for the honour of the law, they were impossible even had they been available. For a time she thought of having Elizabeth disinherited, but desisted when told that Parliament was most unlikely to agree. So Elizabeth survived, as she had a way of doing, while Mary went on with one normal human attachment the fewer, one irritant of fear and jealousy the more, through the increasing isolation of the years left to her.

Within the first of them—only too well within—fell the whole term of her married happiness. In July the English Court journeyed to Southampton to greet the Spanish flotilla bearing its new master, whom Mary at sight found all that she had hoped and more. Everything about him suited her, his trim, well-knit figure scarcely taller than hers, his fair hair and beard and melancholy blue eyes, his grave and deliberate courtesy. Already this last trait had softened the prejudice her suite had brought to the encounter, and nearly melted them altogether when he drained a flagon of the native beer with resolute enjoyment. After the betrothed couple presently left to hold a short semi-private conversation, trying now one language now another as it transpired that Mary's Spanish had grown somewhat rusty, she had no further doubt that Heaven had allotted her the paragon of mankind. A few days later they knelt together in Winchester Cathedral to receive the Bishop's blessing on their nuptials. Four months later they knelt again, together with the Lords and Commons, before Cardinal Pole to receive England's absolution and re-admission into the communion of the Holy Catholic Church. She felt certain by then that she was with child, and Pole's salutation in the terms once used to another Mary by the messenger of God—'Blessed art thou amongst women and blessed is the fruit of thy womb'—scarcely seemed excessive, so brimming over was her heart with happiness and the future with promise.

She had almost exactly four more years to live, years of diminishing hope and joy until nothing was left of either. The severity used against political sedition was turned against religious dissent, often in truth indistinguishable from it, in the futile expectation that a few more examples, a few more rotten limbs cut off and cast into the fire, would at last bring uniformity of belief and peace. The people murmured, became bored or grew

to hate. It was in that mood that they continued to await
with growing scepticism the heir who continued to
put off being born until it became impossible, despite
solemn official assurance, to believe in him at all. Ugly
lampoons were dropped in her way, reflecting on her
honesty and her husband's virility. Even he, when the
normal term had passed, ceased to believe and chafed
to be gone from a land where he was insulted and a
position in the State commensurate with his importance
all but contemptuously denied him. Only Mary, secluded
with her women at Hampton Court, went on clinging
to the conviction that the dropsical swelling in the region
of her womb was actually Philip's child, the heir of
England and the Netherlands, possibly of Spain, the two
Sicilies, the Americas and God knows what else besides.
Finally, in August 1555, even she had to face the truth.
A few weeks later Philip was gone after a parting in
which she gave away nothing to the onlookers of the
moaning agony into which she would collapse as soon
as she was by herself.

Her letters followed him hourly until he set sail from
England, almost daily thereafter. However exhaustive
the budget of public business they referred to his judgment, they continued to carry, as from the beginning,
the burden of her yearning for his presence and her wifely
concern for his well-being, until with pity for her there
begins to mingle a lurking sympathy for him. Yet, for
all the pain and humiliation his prolonged absence caused,
she never directly reproached him but accepted with the
best grace she could his various explanations for putting
off his return. Even when she learned that the sober
young roué was conducting a notorious love affair with
a pretty young countess and running the streets at
midnight with the lighter spirits of Brussels, she kept
the information to herself and vented her grief in private

frenzies which caused those round her who could not help knowing to fear that she was going mad.

He on his side wrote her cool and impersonal letters of comment and advice, not allowing feeling to enter in even where he harboured a sense of personal injury, as in her failure to obtain from Parliament the grant of the Crown Matrimonial to which he felt entitled. One important piece of his advice she might well have taken, namely to stop the burning of the Reformers because of the bad effect it was having on the public mind; a chaplain he had left behind in England even delivered a sermon forcibly putting the same view. But this particular advice Mary felt herself unable to accept. Sacrilege and blasphemy were on the increase and taking forms ever more violent and disgusting; plots were uncovered with dangerous ramifications and were suppressed only to be immediately succeeded by others. In this critical time the first and by far the ablest of her ministers, Gardiner, died suddenly after winning a difficult battle with the Commons for her over supplies, and there was no one to take his place, since her most intimate confidant, Pole—soon to succeed Cranmer as Archbishop of Canterbury—had plainly not been fitted by exile or natural endowment for the active leadership of English politics. As if this were not enough, two consecutive harvests were destroyed by rain and a third for lack of it—calamities sufficiently serious to shake any government and made the more so by placing the country in a position of dependence upon France for its food at a time when relations between the two countries were deteriorating towards open enmity.

The actual declaration of war followed on Philip's return, in March 1557, for a brief, and final, visit of four months after an absence of eighteen. He came this time as King of Spain, his father having abdicated in his favour the previous year. The principal object of his coming was to enlist his wife's aid in the conflict about

to be renewed after a period of truce. The conduct of
France did little to help Mary and her ministers to resist
his plea and safeguard the clause so carefully written into
the marriage contract against just such a contingency,
for the French had given flagrant provocation by subor-
ning English rebels and even abetting some of them in an
attempt to seize the port of Scarborough. So Philip had
his way, and the following August, a month after his
departure, an English contingent assisted him to gain a
crushing victory over his enemy at St. Quentin. But the
French retaliated the following January with a blow even
more telling directed against the English. After a short
siege Calais, England's great continental depôt and the
last remnant of her once vast continental possessions,
capitulated while the English government looked on
helplessly and the English people cried out in rage and
alarm against the inertia, incompetence and treason to
which they more or less justly attributed the famous
citadel's surrender. A determined effort was planned to
recapture it in the spring with Spanish help, but the help
was not forthcoming and the effort was never made.

Few in England had wanted the war, but no one knew
how to get out of it so long as Calais, regarded as vital
to the nation's trade, remained in the enemy's hands.
Trade indeed suffered disastrously; the public credit
sank so low that the Crown was again compelled to offer
interest of 14% and more on loans with which to meet
its current needs. Between the Queen and her subjects
little was left but the bitterness of distrust on the one
side and disaffection on the other; many thought then,
and have thought since, that if the country had not been
in a state of war she might have been driven from her
throne. The fires of persecution, damped down for a
while after consuming Latimer, Ridley and Cranmer
at Oxford and scores of lesser folk in London and the
bishoprics round it, blazed up again to render the thicken-

ing gloom the more visible; as if Mary, like an ecstatic
priestess, had determined that still more sacrifices might
yet placate the God who had so utterly abandoned her.
But the God she worshipped took—had indeed declared
that He took—no pleasure in burnt offerings, even when
their motive was good. The goodness of hers fewer would
perhaps dispute now than formerly, when to be a self-
sufficient unit of power appeared to offer national states
a grander destiny than to remain members under discipline of the whole society of Christendom. But the end
she pursued—though unfortunately not the means by
which she pursued it—was already on its way to being as
outmoded as she herself had become: a tiny, pain-twisted
old woman at 42 with large distraught eyes and fevered
red patches under her wrinkles.

Strange vagaries took hold of her mind as the old
dropsical malady that was to carry her off before the end
of that year gained rapid possession of her body. She
fancied once more that she was with child by Philip,
who had left her so long before, and made provision for
it in the will to which she gave final form the month
before her death. Her thoughts, passing miserably from
Philip to Elizabeth and back again, hit upon the conclusion that Elizabeth was not in fact Henry VIII's
daughter but that Philip had nevertheless fallen in love
with her and would espouse not only her claim to the
throne but herself as soon as he was free. In this last
fantasy there was a certain substance, since Philip was
reported to have shown a keen interest in his sister-in-law
on his previous visit to England, and would in fact
propose for her hand when she was Queen, although it
may be doubted that there was much love involved. But
for Mary it was perhaps proof enough that when she
lay on her death-bed in St. James's Palace her husband,
instead of coming himself as she longed for him to do,
sent one of his Council to press her to acknowledge

Elizabeth as her heir. Wearily she acceded, knowing that the whole nation was fretting for the day when Anne Boleyn's enigmatic, pale-faced daughter would succeed her.

Soon afterwards, in the early morning of 17th November, 1558 she died fortified by the rites of Holy Church: truly and triumphantly fortified, according to those with her at the last. The end was neither painless nor short and the winter's night dragged on long after the administration of the final Sacraments. Her eyes on the Host gleaming in the candlelight, her lips moved in prayer for those she had loved who had suffered for her sake and for those others, no less loved, who had served her so badly; her face the while showing forth her trust in the redeeming merits of her Saviour in an expression of serenity untroubled even by the knowledge that the cause for which she and Pole, who died the evening of that same day, had ineffectually struggled was for the time being beyond saving.

Index